Issues in Historiography

The Debate on the Norman Conquest

Issues in Historiography
General editor
R. C. RICHARDSON
King Alfred's University College

Issues in Historiography

The Debate
on the Norman Conquest

MARJORIE CHIBNALL

**MANCHESTER
UNIVERSITY PRESS**
MANCHESTER AND NEW YORK

The right of Marjorie Chibnall to be identified as the author of this work
has been asserted by her in accordance with the Copyright, Designs and
Patents Act 1988.

Published by Manchester University Press
Oxford Road, Manchester M13 9NR, UK
and Room 400, 175 Fifth Avenue, New York, NY 10010, USA
www.manchesteruniversitypress.co.uk

Distributed exclusively in the USA by
Palgrave, 175 Fifth Avenue, New York NY 10010, USA

Distributed exclusively in Canada by
UBC Press, University of British Columbia, 2029 West Mall,
Vancouver, BC, Canada V6T 1Z2

British Library Cataloguing-in-Publication Data
A catalogue record for this book is available from the British Library

Library of Congress Cataloging-in-Publication Data
A catalog record for this book is available from the Library of Congress

ISBN-10: 0 7190 4913 X

ISBN-13: 978 0 7190 4913 2

First published 1999 by Manchester University Press

First digital, on-demand edition produced by Lightning Source 2006

CONTENTS

GENERAL EDITOR'S FOREWORD

History without historiography is a contradiction in terms. No historian writes in isolation from the work of his or her predecessors nor can the historian stand aloof from the insistent pressures, priorities and demands of the present. Though historians address the past they always do so in ways that are shaped – consciously or unconsciously as the case may be – by the society and systems of their own day and they communicate their findings in ways that are intelligible and relevant to a reading public consisting of their own contemporaries. For these reasons the study of history is concerned not with dead facts and sterile, permanent verdicts but with dialogues, disagreements, and controversies among its presenters, and with the changing methodologies and discourse of the subject over time. *Issues in Historiography* is a series designed to address these issues by means of case studies.

Marjorie Chibnall's guide to the historiography of the Norman Conquest deals with a subject whose constitutional, legal, social, and cultural implications have reverberated down the centuries. The immediate issues and raw nerves expressed in the writings of contemporaries or near contemporaries gave place in time to new stocktakings of the ways in which 1066 represented a dividing line in English history. 'Feudalism' and the 'Norman Yoke' took on added meanings in the heated climate of the seventeenth century for both Royalists and Parliamentarians. Later, in the nineteenth century, the Norman Conquest figured prominently in that neat, linear version of English history often labelled the Whig interpretation. Romantic novelists added colour and picturesque invention to the same story. In our own day the Whig version of the Norman Conquest has been rejected, cataclysmic interpretations of 1066 have been sidelined, and 'Feudalism' is no longer seen as a helpful label. New questions – spurred on by modern experience of, and concern with, social and cultural change, regionalism, gender relations, war, dismantling empires, national identities – are being asked about change and continuity after the Norman Conquest in terms of the law, property and inheritance, women's place in society, the church, and about art and architecture. That so many publications of the 1990s figure in the final chapters demonstrates beyond doubt that this debate – for very different reasons, of course, than the ones which started it – is palpably alive. Cliometrics, counter-factual history, interdisciplinary perspectives, and the linguistic turn in social history now take their place in the long sequence of the historiography of the Norman Conquest alongside Orderic Vitalis, the Bayeux Tapestry, Henry Spelman, J. H. Round, William Maitland, Frank Stenton, and J. C. Holt.

R. C. *Richardson*
January 1999

PREFACE

The invitation to contribute a volume on the Norman Conquest in a series devoted to continuing debates on important historical events has given me an opportunity to review some sixty years of studying and teaching medieval history in Oxford, Southampton, Aberdeen, and since 1947 in Cambridge. It has proved to be a fascinating exercise in seeing how the interpretation of the conquest has changed, as I experienced it while the change was taking place. When I first went up to Oxford in 1933, F. M. Stenton was new and exciting; and V. H. Galbraith as tutor (he had not then published his work on Domesday Book) was even more exciting. In looking back over the next decades I realise how much I have owed to the early giants of the past for the view from their shoulders, even after their heirs, giants too who could see further, had opened up new fields of study. This book is directed in particular to students of history, in the hope that it may help those who are confused by conflicting interpretations, and also that, while appreciating the interpretations of their contemporaries, they will not reject the work of those who in different ways were pioneers and made the new advances possible.

I have many debts to acknowledge. First of all to my Oxford tutor, Evelyn Jamison, who first introduced me to the Normans in Italy (though it was only in 1938, in the abbey church of St Stephen's, Caen, that I realised I must one day work on the men who could build like that); and to Vivian Galbraith, who taught me what history is, and later made it possible for me to fulfil a cherished ambition. This was to edit the *Ecclesiastical History* of Orderic Vitalis, which he accepted for inclusion in his recently launched series of Medieval Texts. He told me when I ventured to make the suggestion that when he first approached Peter Morison of Nelsons to persuade him to publish the series, Morison's immediate reaction had been, 'Find me an editor for Orderic, and I will take your series'. I have a particular debt to John Le Patourel and Jean Yver, with whom I discussed much in the years after 1966, when I took part in the regular meetings of the *Semaine de droit normand*; and also (if I may include one long dead) to Orderic Vitalis, whose marvellous history of the Norman peoples was my constant companion for twenty-five years of editing, and who taught me to see the changes brought about by the Norman Conquest during his lifetime (1075–1141), as they occurred and *before* he knew what the outcome would be; and to understand that this (and not Round's way) was the way to interpret the history of the conquest.

Most recently I have a special debt to my friend Allen Brown, who founded and inspired the Battle Conferences, and to the many other friends with whom I have discussed the late Anglo-Saxon and Anglo-Norman worlds in the stimulating atmosphere of these conferences. They are too numerous to name individually, though I would like to make an exception for Warren Hollister, who founded the conferences run by the Haskins Society in Houston, Texas, and kept alive constant communication between scholars in Great Britain and the USA. Perhaps it is not too much to claim that these two series of conferences have done much to change academic debates from confrontation to consensus.

A number of colleagues have helped me by lending me copies of their works ahead of publication; in particular I thank David Bates, who lent me the proofs of the introduction to his splendid edition of the charters of William the Conqueror between 1066 and 1087. Others are thanked individually in footnotes. Lastly, my special thanks go to the general editor of this series, Professor R. C. Richardson, who has been a constant source of wise guidance and encouragement while the book was being written. My task has been greatly lightened by the helpfulness of the editorial staff at Manchester University Press.

Marjorie Chibnall
Clare Hall, Cambridge

INTRODUCTION

'The Norman Conquest', wrote E. A. Freeman in 1867, 'is the great turning-point in the history of the English nation'.[1] A century and a quarter later, as English history changes in new ways, this statement may need to be modified. Yet 1066, as Sellar and Yeatman discovered, was the one date that every school-child could remember;[2] and even in 1998 public curiosity about the details of the Norman invasion was keen enough to attract the attention of the media in BBC broadcasts and the Sunday newspapers. No list of the decisive battles of the world could justify the omission of the battle of Hastings, with which the effective conquest began. Within a decade historians were busily writing to justify it; and the triumph of the Norman armies inspired in the Bayeux Tapestry a remarkable pictorial account of the invasion. The Hastings campaign was only the beginning; the slow progress of settlement with its initial brutality and later constructive development opened the way for a continuing enquiry into every aspect of the changes in law, social structure, and political expansion. Every age has found in it something relevant to the constitutional, social and cultural issues of its own day, ranging from the political and parliamentary struggles of the seventeenth century through the romantic and scientific interpretations of history in the nineteenth to the debates on colonialism, races, and women's history in the twentieth, and taking in much more. Few subjects provide a more significant touchstone of the way historians in every generation have interpreted the world in which they lived.

Even before the armies met at Hastings, there were well-developed traditions of historical writing in both England and Normandy. In both countries history was largely in the hands of churchmen, particularly monks. England was remarkable in having vernacular records in the various recensions of the *Anglo-Saxon Chronicle*, whereas Norman written history was still in Latin, though more imaginative and less authentic vernacular accounts were provided in the Norman court by the songs of *jongleurs*. Almost from the moment of the invasion historians were at work producing a record of events from the various oral accounts in circulation. What they wrote was influenced initially by well-established historical traditions, including cherished myths; and then, as time passed, by the changing nature of the conquest once it had been followed by settlement.

The earliest Norman chronicles had elaborated a myth of the origins of the Norman people, which stressed the achievements of their leaders from Rollo onwards in welding people of various races into a single Norman people.[3] The Normans, as interpreted in this myth, were united by history, not by blood. In Normandy the conquering northmen had assimilated not only the indigenous Frankish and Gallo-Roman peoples, but also whatever they found most valuable in the established customs and institutions of the land in which they had settled. They expected to do the same in England, where, even though they were proportionately a much smaller element, they were still a very strong conquering minority. It is not surprising that even the conquest of England took many years to complete, and that the partial conquest of Wales, Scotland and Ireland took very much longer.

Settlement, in any case, always changes the behaviour of invaders. The first military phase is marked by violence and often deliberate terrorism, by cruelty and oppression, to force the defeated peoples to surrender. But once the conquerors have established their authority and secured a stake in the country, they become interested in preserving peace and upholding the laws that protect conquered and conquerors alike. This wish is all the stronger when the leader claims, as did William the Conqueror, to be the rightful heir to a kingdom while maintaining his authority over the men he led. Just as the vikings had arrived as rapacious raiders, striking terror into the inhabitants wherever they went, and had settled down to be peaceful and law-abiding members of a community, so the Normans gradually settled into a society where they were able to maintain their authority as much by the laws they enforced as by the military forces they still commanded. The difference can be seen in the changing attitudes of those who wrote in the first two or three decades after 1066, and the next generation of historians, who, through intermarriage and the mingling of customs, were in the process of becoming English, and sometimes wondered just what they were.

In the course of over nine hundred years, interest in the Norman Conquest has depended on the kind of information available to those – whether professional or amateur – who have studied and interpreted the history of the past. The first generation of historians relied primarily on oral information, and almost all were churchmen who wrote in Latin. What they recorded, however, was read aloud in translation to a wider circle of lay readers. In less than a century vernacular histories or romances with a historical colouring were being written down. The most popular histories were lent from one monastic or cathedral library to another and copied; some wealthy people acquired a few books, but the circulation was limited to a relatively small readership.

Among the early Latin histories was the *Deeds of the Norman Dukes*, which was written in Normandy by William of Jumièges in the early 1070s. It gave only a brief account of the events of 1066, but continuations by Orderic Vitalis and Robert of Torigni carried the narrative on to the reign of Henry I. This was a popular book, and was copied many times, particularly in France.[4] The *Deeds of William*, an unfinished biography of the Conqueror by his chaplain, William of Poitiers, was little known in England until the early seventeenth century, when some antiquaries consulted the manuscript in the library of Sir Robert Cotton and it was printed by Duchesne.[5] A Latin poem, the *Song of the Battle of Hastings*, was probably written just after 1066 by Guy, bishop of Amiens, before he came to England in the household of Queen Matilda in 1068. The date and authorship have been hotly debated.[6] Opinion now inclines to the early date; but the historical value of the work is very limited because of the poetic licence freely taken by the author.[7] The *Ecclesiastical History* of Orderic Vitalis, written by an English-born monk who spent the whole of his adult life in Normandy, contains a very full and vivid account of the whole period from 1066 to 1141. Orderic made extensive use of the work of William of Poitiers, and preserved material from the lost chapters. His work was too lengthy for much copying; it was printed in part by Duchesne in the early seventeenth century, but little used until the great edition of Le Prévost and Léopold Delisle was published in Paris (1838–55). By the end of the nineteenth century it was well-known to scholars, and had a strong influence on the accounts of the Normans (and their myth) all over Europe, from Freeman onwards.[8]

Histories written in England were better known in England from the first. The *History of Recent Events* written by Eadmer, an English monk of Canterbury and the biographer of St Anselm, was known in the Middle Ages chiefly through extracts in general histories; but it presented a view of the consequences of the conquest for the English Church. It has been much used since its publication by Martin Rule in the Rolls Series (1884).[9] Both the *Deeds of the Kings* and the *Deeds of the Bishops* of William of Malmesbury were popular books among the literate; his *History of Recent Events*, which chronicled the early years of Stephen's reign, was less copied.[10] William's popularity was, however, largely due to the preservation of extracts in the works of later historians; in particular Ranulf Higden included selected passages in his *Polychronicon* in the early fourteenth century. The *History of the English People* by Henry, archdeacon of Huntingdon, enjoyed similar popularity and similar selective inclusion by Higden in his *Polychronicon*. It too became widely available in the nineteenth century in somewhat inadequate editions. Huntingdon included in his work the early history of the English people up to his own day, and described the post-conquest changes. Consequently his work could be selectively quarried by later writers to provide contradictory views of the effects of the conquest.[11]

The remarkable pictorial record in the Bayeux Tapestry may have been exhibited for a time to a wider public, but its history is a blank until the late fifteenth century, when it was being displayed in the cathedral of Bayeux for the feast day of the relics. Interest in the Tapestry began in England with the work of Andrew Ducarel, who saw it in 1754 and did much to stimulate interest in Norman buildings and ways of life for English readers.[12] Since that time work on the Tapestry and its interpretation has proliferated; Shirley Ann Brown's list of books and articles about it included almost five hundred items published up to 1987.[13]

Not surprisingly, the written Latin narrative sources were known at first only to a very limited readership. The men who read them in manuscript, or even when they first appeared in print, were not numerous, though they were independently minded; the works of men like John Hayward, Robert Brady and Samuel Daniel still make refreshing reading. But the great majority of the population picked up their historical knowledge from the more popular histories, whether poetic and vernacular or traditional and oral. There was always an undercurrent of oral memories, legends and traditional family history, subject to all the weaknesses of the genre, but an important element none the less in shaping the collective memory of the past. By the fifteenth century, when the discovery of printing opened the door to a much wider readership, antiquarians were showing an increasing interest in artefacts, and preparing the way for a critical use of archaeology to add to the written and oral records. And as literacy and education spread, a growing number of people began to investigate the past.

This book will be concerned in the first part with the sources of all kinds for the history of the Norman Conquest, the way they were interpreted as they became more generally available through printing and translation, and the kind of interest they aroused in different people. In addition to those, who have existed throughout all periods, for whom reading and writing history was a 'serious entertainment' or a means of satisfying personal curiosity, there have been many who have turned to it for enlightenment on legal or political matters.

The most potent legacy from the Middle Ages was legal, because the obligations attached to different forms of tenure, particularly military tenure, were part of the daily business of the law courts, Another point of practical interest was personal status and personal freedom. The question of who was entitled to plead in the king's courts in property cases, and who would be sent back to the shrinking but still active manorial courts because (even if he happened to be a wealthy merchant) the plot of village land he held was unfree land, was also of direct interest. It was a short step to ask if the kind of burdens which had become oppressive and archaic were a legacy of the Norman Conquest. So the first reassessments of the conquest came from lawyers and legal historians, who left a stamp on historical interpretation that was to last well into the twentieth century. Combined with past traditions that were sympathetic to the poor and often identified them as English, this produced the theory of the 'Norman yoke' in the seventeenth century, and brought the conquest into questions of social reform. In the past century, as university education has spread, the debate, though still lively, has become both more academic and much wider in scope.

The second part of this book is thematic rather than chronological. It concentrates on the last few decades of the twentieth century, and results from the profound changes that were taking place in political and economic structures and in academic interests and studies. The Second World War left Europe divided physically and ideologically by the Iron Curtain; in it the unitary nation-state no longer seemed the 'natural, inevitable and indeed desirable unit of human power and political organisation'.[14] Ethnic minorities were emerging clamorously even in those states that had escaped restructuring; yet at the same time European movements towards unity and world-wide economic reorganisation demanded a new approach to politics. The Europe of the eleventh and twelfth centuries no longer seemed to be the cradle of the slowly emerging free and democratic nation-states that had been the ideal of nineteenth-century historians. Students of history were more ready to enquire into the ways that power was exercised in that formative period, and to seek the 'history of medieval power in its microcosms'.[15] The reshaping of political structures at that time assumed a contemporary interest.

In the 1960s numerous historians broke away from discussing issues which had dominated earlier academic studies, and which had grown out of the legal and constitutional interests that had first been generated in the law-courts and in political debates, and had become an integral part of university studies. The question of what was meant by 'feudalism' and whether it could ever have been 'imported' seemed no longer relevant. It was replaced by discussions about the nature of lordship, and studies of the varying rates of change in different levels of society. Research and teaching have been helped by critical editions and translations of important sources, including both chronicle and record sources, and the development of sophisticated techniques for studying them. Debates have been stimulated by current historical and political interests, in power and lordship, family and gender, races and peoples, empires and colonies, looser political federations, and general economic movements. Discussions are usually keen and critical, but they are becoming much less confrontational and aim (not always successfully) at finding consensus. The debate is full of contemporary interest, and by no means over.

Notes

1 E. A. Freeman, *The History of the Norman Conquest of England*, 6 vols (Oxford, 1867–79), 1, p. 1
2 W. C. Sellars and R. J. Yeatman, *1066 and All That* (London, 1930, repr. 1975).
3 R. H. C. Davis, *The Normans and their Myth* (London, 1976); G. A. Loud, 'The *Gens Normannorum* – myth or reality?', *Anglo-Norman Studies* 4 (1982), pp. 104–209; Cassandra Potts, '*Atque unum ex diversis gentibus populum effecit*: Historical tradition and the Norman identity', *Anglo-Norman Studies* 18 (1994), pp. 139–52.
4 *Deeds of the Norman Dukes* was not much read in England until Duchesne printed it, together with the works of William of Poitiers and Orderic Vitalis in his *Historiae Normannorum Scriptores Antiquae* (Paris, 1619). Critical study of the numerous manuscripts and recensions did not begin until the nineteenth century, with the work of Léopold Delisle. In 1912 Jean Marx produced a French edition for the Société de l'Histoire de Normandie. An excellent English edition and translation has at last been published by E. M. C. van Houts in the Oxford Medieval Texts: *The 'Gesta Normannorum Ducum' of William of Jumièges, Orderic Vitalis and Robert of Torigni*, 2 vols, Oxford Medieval Texts (OMT) (Oxford, 1992–95).
5 The circulation of William of Poitiers' biography of the Conqueror was very limited, although one manuscript was in England at Ely in the twelfth century. A critical edition did not appear until 1952, when Raymonde Foreville published it with a French translation in *Les Classiques de l'Histoire de France au Moyen Age*. An English edition is now available in the Oxford Medieval Texts: *The 'Gesta Guillelmi' of William of Poitiers*, eds. R. H. C. Davis and M. Chibnall (Oxford, 1998).
6 Arguments in favour of a date *c*.1067 or in the early twelfth century for the poem by Guy, bishop of Amiens, were debated at a Battle Conference in 1979; see R. H. C. Davis, L. J. Engels *et al.*, The *Carmen de Hastingae Proelio*: a discussion', *Proceedings of the Battle Conference on Anglo-Norman Studies* 2 (1980 for 1979), pp. 1–20.
7 The *Song of the Battle of Hastings* was edited for Oxford Medieval Texts in 1972 by Catherine Morton and Hope Muntz; a much-needed revised edition by Frank Barlow is due to be published in the near future.
8 An English edition of Orderic Vitalis with translation was published by M. Chibnall in six volumes in the Oxford Medieval Texts: *The Ecclesiastical History of Orderic Vitalis* (Oxford, 1969–80).
9 *Eadmeri Historia Novorum in Anglia*, ed. Martin Rule, Rolls Series (London,

1984). Eadmer's *Life of St Anselm* has been published with a translation by Richard Southern, in Nelson's Medieval Texts (NMT) (Edinburgh, 1962; repr. in OMT, 1963).

10 Students are still dependent on the Rolls Series texts (hereafter RS) for the De *Gestis Regum Anglorum* of William of Malmesbury, ed. William Stubbs, 2 vols (London, 1887–89); and for his *De Gestis Pontificum Anglorum*, ed. N. E. S. A. Hamilton (London, 1870). The *Historia Novella* was published with a translation in Nelson's Medieval Texts, (ed. K. R. Potter (Edinburgh, 1955); a new edition by Edmund King was published in OMT in 1998.

11 Owing to the number of recensions of the text of the *History of the English* produced by Henry of Huntingdon at different dates, the text history of the work is very complicated. It was first published in part by Sir Henry Savile in 1596; neither this nor any subsequent edition up to and including Thomas Arnold's edition for the Rolls Series (1879) was either complete or satisfactory. The situation has at last been rectified by the magnificent edition produced by Diana Greenway for Oxford Medieval Texts: *Henry, Archdeacon of Huntingdon, 'Historia Anglorum'*, ed. Diana Greenway (Oxford, 1996).

12 See D. J. A. Matthew, 'The English cultivation of Norman History', in *England and Normandy in the Middle Ages*, ed. D. Bates and A. Curry (London, 1995), pp. 1–18, at pp. 11–12.

13 Publications up to 1987 have been listed by Shirley Ann Brown, *The Bayeux Tapestry, History and Bibliography* (Woodbridge, Suffolk, 1988).

14 See below, p. 125.

15 *Cultures of Power: Lordship, Status and Power in Twelfth-Century Europe*, ed. T. N. Bisson (Philadelphia, 1995), pp. 1, 331.

1

The Middle Ages

The first Norman historians of the conquest presented the case for the justice and purpose of the Norman triumph for a small circle of immediate readers, though some had an eye on future generations also. William of Poitiers, a knight turned cleric, who was one of Duke William's chaplains, wrote an unfinished biography of his admired master with an inside knowledge of some of the events, and a determination to show the duke/king's conduct in the best possible light.[1] His book can be seen as a version of the 'official' Norman case for the conquest, which may have been put together to win the support of the pope – and so of the wealthy and powerful Norman Church – for the enterprise.[2] But it was based on close knowledge of the various arguments put forward, and on personal experience of the realities of warfare and the qualities needed for success. The narrative behind the panegyric is a clear statement of what many contemporary Normans believed.

When King Edward the Confessor died childless on 5 January 1066, he left no clear successor, and there were a number of possible claimants. In the absence of any descendant of King Cnut in the direct male line, any Scandinavian claimants were in a weak position. The two strongest contenders were the man on the spot, Harold Godwineson, earl of Wessex, and William, duke of Normandy. Harold could offer no more than an extremely dubious claim to kinship; but he was the wealthiest and most powerful of the earls and the brother of King Edward's wife Edith; and he had a plausible claim to have been designated by King Edward as his successor, both in his lifetime and on his death-bed. Contemporary English sources were inclined to accept his claim.[3] Duke William, however, could claim kinship, since his great-aunt, Emma of Normandy, had been King Edward's mother. During the reign of Cnut, the æthelings – Edward and his younger brother Alfred – had taken refuge in Normandy and been welcomed in the ducal court, where their rights were recognised. Alfred was murdered after an unsuccessful attempt to invade England, and Edward was regarded in Normandy as the lawful heir to the English throne.[4] When Cnut's direct line died out in 1042, Edward returned to England with some Norman backing, and it was widely believed in Normandy that he had designated Duke William as his heir. So contradictory claims existed in England and Normandy before 1066.

The Normans increased their claim in 1064, when Harold Godwineson, on a mission to Normandy – probably to secure the release of two of his kinsmen held as hostages at the Norman court – was shipwrecked off the coast of Ponthieu, taken prisoner by Count Guy, and released only through the intervention of Duke William.[5] The Normans alleged that he had voluntarily become William's vassal and had taken a solemn oath on relics to further his succession. This interpretation was set out shortly after the conquest by William of Poitiers,[6] the Norman monk-chronicler William of Jumièges,[7] and the Bayeux Tapestry.[8] Harold was present at Westminster with all the chief men of the English kingdom when King Edward died, and acted immediately. He was crowned king, with a show of consent which may have been general, the following day.[9]

The succession question was settled within a year by force of arms. Harold's disappointed brother Tostig, who had been forced into exile by rebellions in his former earldom of Northumbria, began to seek friends in Normandy and Scandinavia. First of all he raided round the Isle of Wight and threatened the south coast of England; then he succeeded in coming to an agreement with Harald Hardrada, king of Norway. Hardrada put forward a tenuous claim to the English throne, because of an understanding about the English succession said to have been reached between Cnut's son Harthacnut and Hardrada's kinsman Magnus.[10] Meanwhile during the summer of 1066 Duke William gathered a formidable force of knights from many provinces, and prepared an invasion fleet, while Harold Godwineson anxiously watched the south coast of England, and an English fleet scoured the Channel. In September, when the available food supplies of the English were exhausted and the fleet had withdrawn to the Thames, Hardrada, accompanied by Tostig, struck in Yorkshire, and crushed the local defending forces. Harold Godwineson hurried north to defeat and kill both Hardrada and Tostig at Stamford Bridge.

Immediately Duke William seized his opportunity: within two days of Harold's victory a Norman army had crossed the Channel from Saint-Valéry and disembarked on the Sussex coast between Pevensey and Hastings. The situation has been summed up by David Douglas:

> The full result would not have been attained had not Duke William been able to keep his force in readiness on his side of the Channel longer than did Harold on the south coast of England. If William was enabled to cross the narrow seas unopposed on the night of 27–28 September, and to land on an undefended shore, this was due in large measure to the fact that on 8 September Harold Godwineson had been compelled to disperse his militia, and to send his own ships ... to London.[11]

Even so, Duke William could not have known when he sailed whether he would have to contend with a Scandinavian or an English army.

In the event, it was Harold Godwineson's army that met him on 14 October some miles north of Hastings. During a hard-fought battle, with heavy casualties on both sides, Harold, his brothers Gyrth and Leofwine, and many of the English thegns were among the slain.[12] The Norman army showed the ruthlessness characteristic of invading armies until the remaining English earls and other leaders had abandoned all thoughts of further resistance and made their submission to the conquerors.[13] William was crowned king in Westminster Abbey by Ealdred, archbishop of York, on Christmas Day, 1066, with the acclamation of English and Normans alike. From that time the Norman version of events became the accepted account of the succession.

'His children and grandchildren', wrote William of Poitiers, 'will rule by lawful succession over the English land, which he possesses both by hereditary designation confirmed by the oath of the English, and by right of conquest. He was crowned by the consent, indeed by the wish of the leaders of the same people'.[14] Poitiers accepted the emphasis placed by the Church on the coronation ceremony, and never called Duke William 'king' until after his coronation. The English version of events then went underground. The English people, it has been suggested, were at first too traumatised to attempt to write histories.[15] Some individuals were prepared to make their peace with the invaders and accept the Norman arguments. Queen Edith succeeded in preserving much of her wealth and status as the widow of King Edward; according to William of Poitiers she insisted that her husband had chosen Duke William to be his heir by adoption in place of a son, because he was far worthier of the honour than her brother Harold.[16] There is an early record sympathetic to Harold's claims in the Worcester Chronicle: 'When he [King Edward] was entombed, the underking (subregulus) Harold, son of Earl Godwine, whom the king had chosen before his demise as successor to the kingdom, was elected by the primates of all England to the dignity of kingship, and was consecrated king ... by Ealdred, archbishop of York, on the same day'.[17] But this was a solitary voice. The Norman chroniclers insisted that Harold had been crowned by Stigand, the excommunicated archbishop of Canterbury, and had never been a true king.[18]

One English source written in 1065–67 stands alone: the *Life of King Edward who rests at Westminster*, composed at the request of Queen Edith by an anonymous monk, probably from Saint-Bertin in Flanders. Begun almost certainly when the succession question was still unresolved, and completed in the turmoil immediately following the Norman invasion, it gave a prominent place to the queen, her father Earl Godwine, and her brothers. However, subsequent insertions and omissions, a major rewriting by Ailred of Rievaulx as part of the canonisation process of Edward the Confessor, and a translation into French verse had gradually transformed it by the thirteenth century from a defence of the Godwine family to an emphatic statement of the Norman case, in which Harold was a perjured oath-breaker.[19]

Most of the English chroniclers, like the Normans, accepted that the English had been punished for their sins and Harold's perjury by the just judgment of God.[20] There were protests about Norman oppression, but no attempts to question King William's right to the throne. Any immediate dissension was confined to the later stages of conquest and settlement, and was concerned with the justice or injustice of the ruthless measures adopted by the conquerors. When William of Poitiers wrote in the 1070s, after King William had been forced to spend four years in brutally suppressing revolts in south-west England, the west midlands, the fens, and particularly the north, even he had to acknowledge that the rule of the new king seemed less just to the defeated English than to the Normans. 'And you too, land of England', he wrote, after speaking of Normandy's love for her ruler, 'would love him and hold him in the highest respect ... if, putting aside your folly and wickedness you could learn to judge more soundly the kind of man into whose power you have come'. He went on to denounce Harold's rule as cruel tyranny, and to claim that William had released them from slavery.[21] William of Poitiers accepted the Norman view of Harold's rule as tyrannical and oppressive. It was too early for any defence of Harold to be penned by Englishmen. The eulogy of him as a just and pious ruler, which appears in the Worcester Chronicle, was probably inserted by John of Worcester, when he revised and completed the Chronicle in the twelfth century.[22]

Historians writing in the first decades of the twelfth century were able to see the effects of the conquest in perspective; and those who were of mixed parentage were well aware of conflicting views. Orderic Vitalis, the son of a French priest in the household of Roger of Montgomery and an English mother, was born in Shropshire in 1075, and sent to Normandy as a child oblate to become a monk in the abbey of Saint-Evroult ten years later.[23] He remembered the dispossessed magnates and starving peasants whom he had seen as a child in England.[24] But he also revisited his homeland in 1119, and found the country peaceful and thriving under Henry I. When he wrote his *Ecclesiastical History*, of which a great part is the history of the Norman people, one of his principal sources for this period was the work of William of Poitiers. But Orderic's quotations and allusions were selective: he cut out the passages about King William's justice and mercy towards the English, and stated plainly that many were dispossessed and driven into exile. 'The English', he wrote, 'groaned aloud for their lost liberty and plotted ceaselessly to find some way of shaking off a yoke that was intolerable and unaccustomed'.[25] And when he described the Conqueror's ruthless harrying of the north in 1069, when William – determined to end repeated revolts by a scorched-earth policy – had destroyed the seed corn with the crops and slaughtered the plough oxen along with the other beasts, Orderic's condemnation was unrestrained. He wrote:

> In consequence so terrible a famine fell upon the humble and defenceless populace, that more than 100,000 Christian folk of both sexes, young and old alike, perished of hunger. My narrative has frequently had occasion to praise William, but for this act which condemned the innocent and guilty alike to die by slow starvation I cannot commend him.[26]

Such a deed could be avenged only on the Day of Judgment.

Orderic lived to see England under Henry I after nearly fifty years of Norman rule. Looking at a society that had recovered from the scars of the conquest, he found much to praise:

> King Henry governed the realm ... prudently and well through prosperity and adversity .... In his days every religious order flourished greatly. Monks and clerks increased in number and distinction .... Hermits cut down dense woods and now give praise in the lofty monasteries built in places where formerly robber outlaws used to hide to perform their evil deeds .... He treated the magnates with honour and generosity. He helped his humbler subjects by giving just laws, and protecting them from unjust extortions and robbers.[27]

Another historian of mixed blood, writing slightly later than Orderic, noted both the military ferocity of the Norman Conquest and the beneficial consequences of it. Henry, archdeacon of Huntingdon, wrote a comprehensive *History of the English People*, in which the Norman Conquest was the last of five plagues sent into Britain to punish its sinful people. After the Romans, the Picts and Scots, the Saxons and the Danes, came the Normans, chosen by God to destroy the English people for their serious crimes, because 'the Normans surpassed all other people in their unparalleled savagery'.[28] By 1087 they had fulfilled God's just will, and 'there was scarcely a noble of English descent in England, but all had been reduced to servitude and it was even disgraceful to be called English'.[29] Yet he was prepared to insist that Harold's usurpation of the kingdom had been unlawful.[30] And when he surveyed the whole stretch of history, he considered that the Normans, like the Saxons who had built on what they had gained, and unlike the purely destructive Danes, had suddenly and quickly subdued the land, and had rightly granted the conquered their life, liberty, and ancient laws.[31] The seeming inconsistency is not surprising, since Henry was slowly coming to terms with his own position as a man of mixed blood in a kingdom where conquerors and conquered were gradually becoming assimilated, and the Normans were claiming the English inheritance as their own.[32] William, monk of Malmesbury, another man of mixed parentage, faced the same problem and took a similar line. He was able to reconcile his personal interest in Anglo-Saxon history with his admiration for the work of the Normans by insisting that, in the years before 1066, the English Church had become lax and secularised. Reform had come only with the arrival of the Normans, who had 'breathed new life into religious standards, which had been declining everywhere, so that now you may see churches and monasteries rising in a new style of architecture in all the towns, villages, and country places'.[33]

Consideration of the conquest and its effects was not confined to the writers of Latin chronicles. Administrators and lawyers were daily involved in the practical working-out of the changes. Hagiographers and monks investigating the foundation histories of their houses, laymen and women who commissioned vernacular works – often in poetry – that described the deeds of their ancestors; antiquaries fascinated by buildings no less than early records, all helped to contribute to a varied picture of change over four or five centuries. Oral traditions still kept alive, but severly distorted, events and imagined events that had passed into legend. There was fertile ground in which new interpretations might sprout in the centuries ahead.

While the Norman theory of legitimacy remained in the ascendant, writers of treatises and histories became increasingly preoccupied with the daily practical problems of law. The complicated processes by which Domesday Book was produced in a remarkably short time show the ways in which existing English institutions of shire and hundred, with their reliance on inquest juries, were used by a new Norman aristocracy with different traditions. The Domesday Inquest in 1086 came as the climax of a long series of law-suits to determine rights of possession.[34] Chroniclers were not conscious of this at the time; the realisation came much later. But the law-suits left their mark on many monastic chronicles, such as the Abingdon Chronicle,[35] that described in detail how properties, some of which had been acquired before 1066, were lost or successfully defended. The treatise on the working of the financial system, known as the *Dialogue of the Exchequer*, speculated about some legal changes. Richard fitz Nigel, who wrote it in the reign of Henry II, noted that the *murdrum* fine, originally imposed on villages where a Norman had been violently slain, had been extended to cover all unexplained deaths; he suggested that this was because intermarriage between the English and Norman peoples had made it impossible to distinguish between them. His explanation, whether true or not, was at least plausible.[36]

At the same time, vernacular histories were reaching a wider audience. Geoffrey Gaimar's *Estoire des Engleis* was written at the request of Constance, the wife of Ralph fitz Gilbert, a lady from a second-generation Norman family. Born in England to Norman parents, she was anxious to know more about the history of the English people, to which she felt she belonged. She could read French, but probably not Old English, whereas Gaimar was able to translate the Anglo-Saxon Chronicle as a historical framework for his narrative.[37] Into this he wove legends of heroes, sometimes real like Hereward the Wake, sometimes imagined like Haveloc the Dane, and presented them in rhymed French with all the trappings of the chivalric epics dear to the Normans.[38] In his general theme he was in complete agreement with the Latin chroniclers: Duke William's conquest was a just assertion of right. At the same time the rebels were handled sympathetically: Hereward's rebellion was presented as a protest against his unjust disinheriting.[39] In this Gaimar picked up one of the legends about Hereward which were in general circulation, and were to be incorporated later in the Latin *Gesta Herewardi*.[40] There was material here for some later readers to suspect Norman ruthlessness.

Later vernacular histories claimed some royal patronage.

Henry II possibly encouraged Wace, author of the *Roman de Rou* in which the deeds of the first Norman conqueror, Rollo, and his descendants are described. Wace was certainly rewarded with a prebend in Bayeux; later the king transferred his favour to Benoît of Sainte-Maure.[41] Such histories continued the Norman genealogical tradition, but went beyond the exploits of the dukes to describe the valiant deeds performed by ancestors of the authors' aristocratic patrons, particularly in the conquest of England. While Wace certainly had sound information about the families he knew in the region of Caen and Bayeux,[42] he included among the participants in the battle of Hastings men who did not come to England until later. This was to lead to a greatly inflated list of 'Companions of the Conqueror', drawn up in the nineteenth century.[43]

Wace's other main work, the *Roman de Brut*, belongs rather to romance than to history. It gave a version in rhyming French of the Brutus legend, most fully expounded by Geoffrey of Monmouth in his Latin *History of the Kings of Britain*.[44] At the time that the 'English' were discovering their new identity in the 1130s, Geoffrey provided them with the type of origin-legend that Dudo of Saint-Quentin had provided for the Normans over a century earlier. He traced the earliest British kings to a legendary Brutus, said to be the great-grandson of Aeneas.[45] Geoffrey's book was about the British kings, mostly legendary, from the twelfth century BC to the death of Cadwallader in the seventh century AD; but the English fitted the genealogy onto their own kings. Geoffrey embroidered, enlarged, and added to their most cherished legends, and in particular recounted stories of King Arthur and the prophecies of Merlin. These prophecies were the only part of the book that had any connection with the Norman Conquest: Geoffrey, writing at the time of the Angevin struggle for the throne and favouring their cause, included some easily identifiable references to recent history in the prophecies.[46]

The *Brut* was rewritten, expanded, and translated into both French and English in a number of versions in the thirteenth and fourteenth centuries.[47] It was immensely popular. Many serious historians accepted parts at least as reliable. Henry of Huntingdon, who saw it at Bec-Hellouin after he had finished writing the second version of his own history, added a new chapter to include selected material from it.[48] For at least four centuries much of the material was accepted by a wide range of readers, and sceptics met with scorn from the true believers. Its popularity is an early illustration of the way in which the intellectual sub-culture of historical romance was liable to intrude into more critical history down to recent times and including at least the nineteenth century.

Among the Latin histories written by monks from the twelfth century onwards, the official version of William the Conqueror's just succession to the throne of King Edward was preserved as a dominant theme, even when some of his actions were condemned (as they had been by many of his contemporaries). Many monastic annals and chronicles combined accounts of the foundation and endowment of the author's monastery, together with more general history.[49] In some houses research in archives and earlier histories was active, and the miscellaneous materials could easily suggest different interpretations. King William might appear as a respected church patron and benefactor, while anyone dipping selectively into different parts of the history that Henry of Huntingdon wrote and revised through thirty years of changing circumstances could sometimes find the king called tyrannical, or the Normans denounced for their savagery. It is hardly surprising that ambivalence can be found in the work of Matthew Paris, the most versatile, imaginative and well-read of the thirteenth-century historians who contributed to the fame of historical writing at St Albans.[50] And a perennial problem was the meaning of the word 'English'. Matthew Paris's appreciation of the artistic achievements of the 'English' before 1066 referred to Anglo-Saxon traditions; he implied a different kind of Englishness when he attacked the foreigners – not Normans, but Poitevins and Angevins – who were being promoted over the heads of the 'English' of his own day (who included descendants of Normans).[51]

Matthew's ambivalence is an example of the way in which even the Latin chroniclers who accepted the official version of the Norman Conquest were aware of the popular traditions that had kept alive legends of heroic English resistance. Rebecca Reader commented on Matthew's *Estoire de Saint Aedward le Roi*:

The *Estoire* constitutes an oasis of pro-English feeling drawing upon a rich mixture of hagiographical adulation of the English royal line and surreptitious disapproval of the Norman invaders .... It is paradoxical that a monk openly favouring William's cause in 1066, and strongly condemning Harold's perjury, is a mine of pro-English sympathies rich in adulation of Anglo-Saxon monarchy and pervaded by tacit criticism of Norman moral virtue.[52]

Indeed, in spite of intermarriage between Norman and English landholders, and the assumption of the second- and third-generation settlers that they were English, a tendency persisted in popular writings to describe all oppressive or wealthy rulers and administrators as Norman, and all poor and oppressed people as English.

The veneration of the Old English saints aroused mixed reactions from the time of the conquest onwards. Lives of the saints were adapted to local cults; but all kept the official version of the conquest itself, even when extolling the virtues of the saintly English kings. *The Life of King Edward* (the Confessor), which had been written in Latin by Ailred of Rievaulx, was one of the *Lives* translated into French verse by Matthew Paris.[53] In its final form it incorporated new material, which further denigrated Harold as a perjured tyrant who had even crowned himself king; an illustration in the earliest manuscript, probably written by Matthew himself, shows him placing the crown on his own head.[54] Cults which might easily have become seditious were kept under cover. The canons of Waltham, a college of secular clerks founded by Harold that claimed to be his burial-place, discouraged any cult at his tomb, though the Waltham chronicler was one of the very few who praised Harold unreservedly.[55] A number of cults, which would hardly have survived the much more careful scrutiny being encouraged at Rome, were questioned: some of Evesham's more dubious relics were even submitted to the ordeal by fire. Yet by the beginning of the twelfth century the English themselves were as ready as the Normans to discard their least cherished cults; and those with strong local support either survived or were reinstated after a short break. The great monasteries in particular held resolutely to the cult of their most revered saints.[56] For the most part the veneration of pre-Conquest saints continued without interruption, and presented no threat to the Norman rulers. Indeed a powerful royal saint like St Edmund, king and martyr (*d.* 870), was readily adopted by the first Norman kings as their predecessor and protector.[57]

New types of history flourished in the later Middle Ages, including town chronicles and antiquarian histories that appealed to a widening circle of literate readers.[58] At the same time, traditional monastic chronicles, based on the work of twelfth-century historians, continued to be written. Their authors, with the omnivorous tastes characteristic of medieval writers, were often prepared to incorporate stories from Geoffrey of Monmouth and the *Brut*, alongside extracts from William of Malmesbury and Henry of Huntingdon. Ranulf Higden, monk of Chester, produced the most popular history of all in his *Polychronicon*.[59] An enormous work, it had some of the characteristics of a popular encyclopaedia, and began with an account of the universe and the countries of the world. Higden made some critical use of Geoffrey of Monmouth, whom he admired. He enjoyed Geoffrey's stories, and was prepared to take over his account of the origins of three archbishoprics in England in the time of Lucius, a legendary first Christian king. This distortion of Bede was to provide ammunition for the royal servants who later attempted to justify Henry VIII's break from Rome. In a more critical spirit, Higden asked why King Arthur was not mentioned by either Gildas or Bede.[60]

On the main theme of the legitimacy of the Norman Conquest, Higden stood firmly in the accepted tradition. He made, however, some personal comments, derived from his own observation of the world around him, about the linguistic consequences of the coming of the Normans:

> It is clear that there are as many different languages as peoples in this island. The Scots, however, and the Welsh, in so far as they have not intermixed with other nations, have retained the purity of their native speech .... The Flemish who live in the west of Wales have abandoned their barbarous speech, and speak Saxon well enough. Likewise the English although in the beginning they had a language of three branches, namely southern, midland and northern, as coming from three Germanic peoples, nevertheless as a result of the mixture, first with the Danes and then Normans, by a corruption of

their language in many respects, they now incorporate strange bleat-
ings and babblings. There are two main causes for their present
debasement of the native language, one, that children in the schools
... are compelled since the coming of the Normans to abandon their
own tongue and to construe into French, and, secondly, that children of the nobility are taught French from the cradle and rattle.
Because of this peasants wishing to be similar ... make every effort
to Frenchify their speech. It is a remarkable thing that in one little
land the native language of the English should be pronounced in so
many different ways, while the language of the Normans, which was
imported, is so uniform.[61]

When John Trevisa translated the *Polychronicon* into English in
1385, he added a note to explain that by that time the custom of
teaching French had been changed, and that 'in all the grammar
schools children leave French and construe and learn in English,
and have an advantage on one side and a disadvantage on the
other'. The advantage was that they learned grammar more
quickly, and the disadvantage that they knew so little French that
they were handicapped if they went overseas. He added that
gentlemen too had given up teaching their children French.[62]

Higden and Trevisa were commenting on what they saw and
heard, not passing judgement on the Normans; but there was
material for later writers to assert that King William had tyranni-
cally imposed the French language on the conquered English.
Their works enjoyed lasting popularity. The *Polychronicon* was
very widely disseminated in all the great religious centres, and in
colleges and hospitals; some individual clerics too owned copies.
As was to be expected, laymen were the principal owners of
Trevisa's translation.[63] In 1480–82 Caxton chose the *Polychronicon* and the *Brut* as the first historical works to be printed,
and both books became more widely accessible.[64]

Other thirteenth- and fourteenth-century chroniclers, writing
in Middle English verse, commented on the linguistic differences,
with French the speech of the gentry and English that of the peasantry. They gave a new twist in their references to the Norman
Conquest. Whereas Robert of Gloucester merely noted that the
land had passed into the hands of the Normans, who were the
'high men' while the Saxons were the 'low men',[65] Thomas of
Castleford (writing *c.*1327) expressed more feeling:

> Fra Englisse blood Englande he [William] refte,
> Na maner soil with them he lefte ....
> Dwelle they shall alls bondes and thralles,
> And do all that to thraldom falles.[66]

In this way he linked serfdom with English blood, and attributed the misfortunes of the English to the taking of their land by the Normans. Robert Mannyng, whose *Chronicle* was completed before 1338, used still stronger language:

> Sithen he [William] and his haf had the lond in heritage
> That the Inglis have so lad that they live in servage;
> He sette the Inglis to be thralle, that or was so fre.[67]

Thomas of Castleford was a Yorkshire cleric, and Robert Mannyng was a canon of Sixhills, who translated and augmented the earlier French chronicle of Peter of Langtoft.[68] Both were living at a time of acute economic crisis, accompanied by storms, epidemics, famine and civil disturbance.[69] Their observation of peasant hardship and distress, added to the clearly audible fact that English was the language of the poor, whatever their racial origins, whereas it was only one of two or three languages for the better-off, and taken together with statements in earlier chronicles about the seizure of land by the Norman aristocracy, could have led them to suppose that the Normans had enslaved and impoverished the English. They do not appear to imply lasting racial tensions. But they provided material for a view of English and Norman disharmony that could later resurface in another guise.[70]

The writings of the later Middle Ages show that after four centuries, men and women looking at the world around them were most aware of possible consequences of the Norman Conquest through language and law. In the law courts the reality of the Norman Conquest was continually brought home to litigants. The common law, as it was slowly built up in England, was essentially pragmatic, based on precedent, and continually developing. During the settlement of land claims in the aftermath of the conquest, 1066 had been used as one possible date for establishing legitimate tenure. Change came slowly: even though first 1135 and later 1189 began to supersede it as the limit of legal memory it was not until the end of the thirteenth century that

1066 disappeared altogether. Church landlords were among the last to defend their claims by alleging pre-conquest tenure of property.[71] In special cases Domesday Book might be consulted, particularly in the pleas brought by peasants who claimed to be 'sokemen of the ancient demesne', and as such entitled to plead in the royal courts from which villeins were excluded. In such cases Domesday Book might be invoked to prove whether the land in question had been royal demesne in the time of Edward the Confessor.[72]

Most frequently, however, for men and women of all classes, cases involving the dues and services of both military and non-military tenures were a potential reminder of the practical implications of tenure, which permeated the whole of society. In a common bench case of 1286 concerning the taking of animals from a holding of which the lordship was challenged, the legal record departs from law French to include the judge's citation of a proverbial saying in Middle English, 'where you have a man you have a lord'.[73] And lordship, whether rightly or wrongly, was becoming associated with the conquest. Dues and services that were tenurial became a constant source of litigation and irritation. Legal records stored up potentially explosive interpretations of the effects of the Norman Conquest. For the time being, however, they were important for fostering a method of thought; their possibly subversive implications were not fully realised until the seventeenth century.

In spite of the mingling of peoples and cultures that took place in the century after the Norman Conquest, memories of the disaster and of the loss it caused in its immediate aftermath survived in two forms. One was the often mechanical copying of entries from one chronicle to another, particularly in the short, fragmentary monastic annals tucked away in monastic cartularies, which preserved in writing the bitter comments characteristic of the *Anglo-Saxon Chronicle*. When the fourteenth-century monk of Lilleshall inserted the opening sentences of a chronicle among the miscellaneous documents at the end of a cartulary, he accepted the official story of William I's legitimate conquest, but added laconically that, on his return from Normandy in 1067, he 'divided the land of England among his knights at his will'.[74] Such a statement, whatever its original intention, could be read by later

researchers as implying a kleptocracy. Other brief chronicle statements probably recorded the real bitterness and loss of the
dispossessed as it was preserved in popular memory. Such were
the statements in the Welsh chronicles that the Normans had
been guilty of 'unbearable tyranny, injustice and oppression',
which, as R. R. Davies wrote, refuelled resentment in each generation.[75] Medieval sources provided a rich supply of material for
all kinds of interpretations and misinterpretations by later
writers.

Notes

1 The 'Gesta Guillelmi' of William of Poitiers, eds R. H. C. Davis and Marjorie
   Chibnall, OMT (Oxford, 1998): hereafter William of Poitiers.
2 George Garnett, 'Coronation and propaganda: some implications of the
   Norman claim to the throne of England in 1066, TRHS (Transactions of the
   Royal Historical Society), 5th ser., 36 (1986), pp. 91–116, at pp. 110–11.
3 The Anglo-Saxon Chronicle, eds D. Whitelock, D. C. Douglas and S. Tucker
   (London, 1961); The Chronicle of John of Worcester OMT (Oxford, 1995),
   2, pp. 598–601.
4 Simon Keynes, 'The Æthelings in Normandy', Anglo-Norman Studies 13
   (1991), pp. 173–205.
5 William of Poitiers, pp. 68–71; The 'Gesta Normannorum Ducum' of William
   of Jumièges, Orderic Vitalis and Robert of Torigni, ed. E. M. C. van Houts, 2
   vols, OMT (Oxford, 1992–95), 2. pp. 158–61 (hereafter William of
   Jumièges); The Bayeux Tapestry, ed. Sir Frank Stenton (London, 1957), pls
   1–30.
6 William of Poitiers, pp. 70–1.
7 William of Jumièges, pp. 160–1.
8 Bayeux Tapestry, pl. 29.
9 Anglo-Saxon Chronicle (E) s.a. (sub anno, i.e. under the year) 1066; John of
   Worcester, 2, p. 600; William of Poitiers, p. 100 and n.1.
10 David C. Douglas, William the Conqueror (London, 1964), pp. 164, 173.
11 Douglas, William the Conqueror, p. 195.
12 William of Poitiers, pp. 126–39; Bayeux Tapestry, pls 54–73; R. A. Brown,
   'The Battle of Hastings', Anglo-Norman Studies 3 (1980), pp. 1–21; Stephen
   Morillo, Warfare under the Anglo-Norman Kings (Woodbridge, Suffolk,
   1994), pp. 163–8.
13 Ann Williams, The English and the Norman Conquest (Woodbridge, Suffolk,
   1995); Anglo-Saxon Chronicle (D) s.a.1066, 1067; M. Strickland, 'Military
   technology and conquest: the anomaly of Anglo-Saxon England', Anglo-
   Norman Studies 19 (1997), pp. 353–82 at pp. 372–3.
14 William of Poitiers, p. 151.
15 E. M. C. van Houts, 'The memory of 1066 in written and oral tradition',
   Anglo-Norman Studies 19 (1997), pp. 167–79.
16 William of Poitiers, pp. 114–15.

17 *John of Worcester*, pp. 600–601; this may, however, be an early twelfth-century addition. The editors (p. 600, n.2) point out that verses in *The Anglo-Saxon Chronicle (C, D) s.a.*1065 and *(E) s.a.*1066 suggest that Harold was Edward's choice; and this is also stated by Eadmer, *Historia Novorum in Anglia*, ed. Martin Rule, RS (London, 1884), p. 8.

18 *Anglo-Saxon Chronicle (E) s.a.*1066; *William of Poitiers*, pp. 150–1 (who does not actually name the archbishop of York); *The Ecclesiastical History of Orderic Vitalis*, ed. M. Chibnall, 6 vols, OMT (Oxford, 1969–80), 2, p. 182 (hereafter *Orderic Vitalis*).

19 See *The Life of King Edward who rests at Westminster*, 2nd edn, ed. Frank Barlow, OMT (Oxford, 1992); Pauline Stafford, *Queen Emma and Queen Edith* (Oxford, 1997), pp. 14, 275.

20 *William of Poitiers*, pp. 114–15; Henry, *Archdeacon of Huntingdon, 'Historia Anglorum'*, ed. D. Greenway, OMT (Oxford, 1996), pp. 338–9, 384–7 (hereafter *Henry of Huntingdon*).

21 *William of Poitiers*, pp. 156–9.

22 *John of Worcester*, 2, p. 600, n.3.

23 *Orderic Vitalis*, 2, pp. xiii–xiv, 202–5; 3, pp. 6–9.

24 M. Chibnall, *The World of Orderic Vitalis* (Oxford, 1984; repr. Woodbridge, Suffolk, 1996), pp. 12–13.

25 *Orderic Vitalis*, 2. pp. 202–3.

26 *Ibid.*, 2, pp. 232–3.

27 *Ibid.*, 5, pp. 294–7.

28 *Henry of Huntingdon*, pp. 338–9.

29 *Ibid.*, pp. 402–3.

30 *Ibid.*, pp. 385–7.

31 *Ibid.*, pp. 272–3.

32 See below, pp. 127–9.

33 William of Malmesbury, *De Gestis Regum Anglorum*, ed. W. Stubbs, 2 vols, RS (London, 1887–89), pp. 2, 306.

34 See below, pp. 92–3.

35 *Chronicon Monasterii de Abingdon*, ed. J. Stevenson, 2 vols, RS (London, 1858).

36 Richard fitz Nigel, *Dialogus de Scaccario*, ed. Charles Johnson; corr. F. E. L. Carter and D. E. Greenway, OMT (Oxford, 1983), pp. 52–3.

37 Ian Short, 'Patrons and polyglots: French literature in twelfth-century England', *Anglo-Norman Studies* 14 (1992), pp. 229–49, at pp. 237, 243, 244; John Gillingham, 'Kingship, chivalry and love. Political and cultural values in the earliest history written in French: Geoffrey Gaimar's *Estoire des Engleis*', *Anglo-Norman Political Culture in the Twelfth-Century Renaissance*, ed. C. Warren Hollister (Woodbridge, Suffolk, 1997), pp. 33–58, at pp. 33–8.

38 G. Gaimar, *L'Estoire des Engleis*, ed. A. Bell (Oxford, 1960).

39 Gaimar, *Estoire*, lines 5461–5.

40 Hugh Thomas, 'The *Gesta Herewardi*: the English and their conquerors', forthcoming in *Anglo-Norman Studies*, 1999.

41 Van Houts, 'The memory of 1066', pp. 178–9; Short, 'Patrons and polyglots', p. 237.

42 E. M. C. van Houts, 'Wace as historian', in *Family Trees and the Roots of Politics*, ed. K. S. B. Keats-Rohan (Woodbridge, Suffolk, 1997), pp. 103–32; M. Bennett, 'Poetry as history? *The Roman de Rou* of Wace as a source for the Norman conquest', *Anglo-Norman Studies 5* (1983), pp. 21–39.

43 D. C. Douglas, 'Companions of the Conqueror', *History* 28 (1943), pp. 129–47.

44 Geoffrey of Monmouth, *Historia Regum Britanniae*, ed. Neil Wright (Cambridge, 1986); Antonia Gransden, *Historical Writing in England, c.1307 to the Early Sixteenth Century* (London and Henley, 1982), pp. 73–7, 222–3.

45 *Henry of Huntingdon*, pp. 558–9, summarises Geoffrey's account of the Brutus legend.

46 Geoffrey of Monmouth, *The History of the Kings of Britain*, trans. Lewis Thorpe (Harmondsworth, Middlesex, 1966), pp. 170–85. Orderic Vitalis included the parts of the prophecies that seemed to apply to his own time in his *Ecclesiastical History* (See *Orderic Vitalis*, 6, pp. 381–9). The 'Lion of Justice' was popularly identified with Henry I.

47 John Taylor, *The 'Universal Chronicle' of Ranulf Higden* (Oxford, 1966), pp. 13–16.

48 *Henry of Huntingdon*, pp. ci–cii.

49 Antonia Gransden, *Historical Writing in England, c.550–1307* (London, 1974), ch. 13.

50 See Rebecca Reader, 'Matthew Paris and the Norman Conquest', in *The Cloister and the World: Essays in Medieval History in Honour of Barbara Harvey*, ed. John Blair and Brian Golding (Oxford, 1996), pp. 118–47.

51 *Ibid.*, pp. 138–45.

52 *Ibid.*, pp. 140–1.

53 *The Life of King Edward who rests at Westminster*, 2nd edn, ed. F. Barlow, OMT (Oxford, 1992), pp. xxxviii–xlvi.

54 Cambridge University Library, MS ee 3.59, p. 56.

55 *The Waltham Chronicle*, ed. L. Watkiss and M. Chibnall, OMT (Oxford, 1994), pp. xiv, xlv–xlvi, 56–7.

56 S. J. Ridyard, '*Condigna veneratio*: post-conquest attitudes to the saints of the Anglo-Saxons', *Anglo-Norman Studies 9* (1987), pp. 179–206, at pp. 187–9. The present state of the debate is well described by Paul Hayward, 'Post-conquest attitudes to the saints of Anglo-Saxon England', forthcoming in *Anglo-Norman Studies*, 1999.

57 Ridyard, '*Condigna veneratio*', pp. 187–8; cf. R. Folz, *Les Saints Rois du Moyen Age en Occident* (Brussels, 1984), p. 193.

58 Gransden, *Historical Writing from c.1307*, chs 8, 11.

59 *Polychronicon Ranulphi Higden*, eds Churchill Babington and J. R. Lumly, 9 vols, RS (London, 1865–86).

60 *Polychronicon*, 2, pp. 110–18; Taylor, *Ranulf Higden*. pp. 44–5, 167–8; see below, pp. 29–30.

61 *Polychronicon*, 2, pp. 156–62; Taylor, *Ranulf Higden*, pp. 168–9.

62 *Polychronicon*, 2, p. 161; Taylor, *Ranulf Higden*, p. 61.

63 Taylor, *Ranulf Higden*, pp. 105–9, 151.

64 *Ibid.*, pp. 140–1,

65 *The Metrical Chronicle of Robert of Gloucester*, ed. W. A. Wright, 2 vols, RS (London, 1887), lines 7498–501.

66 Thomas of Castleford, *Chronicle,* in *An Old and Middle English Anthology*, ed. Rolf Kaiser, 3rd edn (Berlin, 1958), pp. 364–5, lines 31925–6, 31935–6.

67 Robert Mannyng, *The Chronicle of Robert Mannyng of Brunne*, ed. F. J. Furnivall, 2 vols, RS (London, 1887), 2, p. 8.

68 The disharmony of English and Normans expressed in these passages is discussed by T. Turville-Petre, 'Politics and poetry in the early fourteenth century', *The Review of English Studies*, n.s. 39 (1988), pp. 1–28; D. Moffat, 'Sin, conquest, servitude: English self-image in the chronicles of the early fourteenth century', in *The Work of Work,* eds A. J. Franzen and D. Moffat (Glasgow, 1994), pp. 146–68.

69 E Miller and J. Hatcher, *Medieval England: Rural Society and Economic Change, 1086–1348* (London and New York, 1978), pp. 58–63; I. Kershaw, 'The great famine and agrarian crisis in England, 1315–22', *Past and Present* 59 (1973), pp. 3–50.

70 See below, pp. 23–4, 53–4.

71 Paul Brand, '"Time out of mind": the knowledge and use of the eleventh- and twelfth-century past in thirteenth-century litigation', *Anglo-Norman Studies* 16 (1994), pp. 37–54.

72 Paul Hyams, *King, Lords and Peasants in Medieval England* (Oxford, 1986), pp. 63–5; R. S. Hoyt, *The Royal Demesne in English Constitutional History, 1066–1272* (Ithaca, New York, 1950), pp. 194–8; M. K. McIntosh, 'The privileged villeins of the Ancient Demesne', *Viator* 7 (1976).

73 *The Earliest English Law Reports*, ed. Paul A. Brand, 2 vols, Selden Society (London, 1995–96), 2, p. 256.

74 *The Cartulary of Lilleshall Abbey*, ed. Una Rees, Shropshire Archaeological and Historical Society (1997), p. 164, no. 323.

75 R. R. Davies, *Conquest, Coexistence and Change: Wales, 1063–1415* (Oxford, 1987), p. 100.

2

From the Reformation to the Restoration: the widening of the debate

The invention of printing and the spread of literacy among educated laymen led to an outburst of historical and antiquarian interest. It was further stimulated by the flood of manuscripts from monastic libraries that found their way into the collections of nobles, new colleges, churchmen such as Archbishop Parker, and newly-enriched country gentlemen after the Dissolution of the Monasteries. The first general histories in the English language were translations of medieval Latin and French works, notably Higden and the *Brut*. Very soon original English histories began to appear in print; and at the same time there were still enough learned humanist scholars to appreciate Polydore Vergil's *Anglica historia* in Latin. French survived only in the peculiar legal French of the law courts, equally far removed from both the language of Paris and that of Stratford-atte-Bowe.

Much of the material in the new general histories came from the works of well-known writers such as William of Malmesbury and Henry of Huntingdon, and was roughly cobbled together, with a mixture of legends and epic accounts of battles. These suited the needs of the time, which were first of all a longing for stability and strong government after the wars of Lancaster and York, and later a genuine love of country and pride in its achievements.[1] The most contentious issue at first was religion. So writers of history emphasised legitimate royal power and the continuity of royal rights since the remote past. Delving into earlier history to resolve present difficulties, they found evidence to support royal rather than papal supremacy in Church government during the critical years before the break from Rome. There was much in the medieval attitude to the Norman Conquest that appealed to Tudor historians; until the end of the sixteenth century most of them, as a result of accepting the politically correct language of the day, had no difficulty in avoiding suspicion of treason and detention in the Tower.

Most of the works of general history were neither critical nor well-written; they were a hotch-potch of chronicle information, legend, and sheer invention. Holinshed's bold claim that chronicles carried the greatest credit after Holy Writ was certainly not justified by the mixture of raw chunks of chronicle and pure myth that he and many of his colleagues compiled.[2] They are, however evidence of the value set on history: of the conviction that present rights and wrongs had their roots in the past, and that the past could help to provide solutions for present problems. A few writers, notably Polydore Vergil, were critical. He found Geoffrey of Monmouth wholly untrustworthy and rejected the legends of Brutus with his Trojans.[3] His work, written in a deliberately literary style, was for the elite. Most other historians were more credulous, or sometimes more unscrupulous.

The group of scholars who, under Edward Foxe, diligently put together materials to justify Henry VIII's supremacy in both Church and State were prepared to accept anything that served their purpose. Foxe used a spurious collection of early English laws to demonstrate that King Lucius I (a fictional character occurring in Geoffrey of Monmouth's history) had become the first Christian ruler of Britain in 187 AD, and had endowed the British Church with all its liberties and possessions, whereas the pope had merely endorsed this grant. King Henry evidently accepted this story, and believed England to have been an empire independent of any other authority since the early British past.[4] Whether Foxe himself believed it is by no means certain. It gave him the precedent he needed, and with such an ancient and sweeping privilege (however improbable) in his dossier he did not need to investigate any minor changes that might have occurred at the time of the Norman Conquest. In a later and more far-reaching work, the famous *Book of Martyrs*, John Foxe assembled a motley collection of extracts from early records and innumerable legends to support a thesis that 'the proud and misordered reign of Antichrist began to stir in the Church of Christ' about the time of the Norman Conquest.[5] But the suggestion that the early Church in England had enjoyed a freedom from Rome that was undermined by the Norman kings did not have its day until very much later.

Some historians looked back to the Norman period in search of precedents for a succession problem that became acute in the mid-sixteenth century. When Henry I realised that he might die without a legitimate male heir, he had tried to secure the succession for his daughter Matilda, married to Count Geoffrey of Anjou as her second husband. Though Matilda never succeeded in gaining the crown for herself, and had to be content with securing it for her son Henry II, she established a precedent for the transmission of the crown by a woman. Sixteenth-century historians interpreted events in the terms familiar to them. Writing at a time when important constitutional matters were debated in Parliament, Holinshed believed that King Henry I had called a parliament, and by its authority had caused his daughter 'to be established as his lawful successor, with an article of entail upon her issue';[6] – a free interpretation of the council in which Henry had induced his magnates to swear to accept Matilda and her infant children. For Holinshed, as for Foxe on the question of royal supremacy in the Church, history could be consulted for evidence of rights, which could then be established and defined by legislation in Parliament.

Legally-minded scholars had a different view of the past; some deplored the changes introduced after the conquest in law and language. In his *Dialogue between Pole and Lupset* (written in the 1530s) Thomas Starkey attributed to Pole a demand to shake off the 'tyrannical customs and unreasonable bonds' imposed by the Conqueror 'when he subdued our country and nation'. He argued specifically against the feudal burdens of wardship and marriage, complained that the common law was written, disputed, and taught in French, to the dishonour of the English nation, and argued for a reception of Roman civil law.[7] Pole's alleged plea for the civil law was a by-product of the humanist studies of the time, and was not to persist. But the use of French in the law courts continued to attract complaints; resentment at the legal and financial burdens attached to military tenure, and wider, more constitutional problems of the effect of the conquest on the royal power were to be debated at greater length by lawyers and politicians for over a century, before being taken over by philosophers.

In non-controversial matters the Norman Conquest, though not treated as generally oppressive or unjust, was almost invariably regarded as a significant date. Writers of general histories who broke up their narrative into periods, began a new era in 1066. This might be marked simply by the beginning of a new volume, as in Holinshed's history. Alternatively the 'fantastic work entitled *Albion's England*', written in atrocious doggerel by William Warner in 1602, emphasised the conquest as a great divide. Warner urged his Muse to persist:

> and tell, How by the *Norman Conquest* here an other world befell: New Lawes ... came in,
> New Lords also, at whom, for most our auncient Crests begin,
> The *English* sinke, the *Normans* swimme, all topsie-turvie was,
> Untill the Conqueror had brought his whole command to pass'.[8]

This contrast between English and Normans was made, however, in the spirit of reconciliation characteristic of the time. Warner's main purpose in mentioning the two peoples was to stress the ultimate mingling of Norman and English blood in the person of Henry II; he may have mentally drawn a parallel to the union of York and Lancaster in the person of Henry VIII.

If Warner's work represented, as McKisack claimed, 'what our history looked like to the ordinary man',[9] then the 'ordinary man' did not include the country gentlemen with antiquarian interests educated in the Inns of Court. Aided by the plunder from the monasteries, some of these men amassed libraries very much more substantial than the modest handful of books that had made Geoffrey Gaimar's patron appear conspicuously well-read in the twelfth century.[10] An inventory taken in 1556 of the library of one well-to-do gentleman, Sir William More JP, of Loseley House in Surrey, shows the width of his interests. Among some 140 volumes were works on surveying, geometry, cosmography, the treatment of horses, the names of those paying for knights' fees in Surrey, statutes of the realm from the earliest times, treatises on legal matters and formularies, as well as histories and books for recreation.[11] For many the interest of their studies lay in equipping themselves to act responsibly as landowners and justices of the peace, and in tracing the histories of their families and the origin of their family crests. As J. H. Round commented much later, 'the nobility and gentry and all who aspired to their rank were pedigree mad'.[12] Such people often read their general history uncritically: political speculation could be dangerous.

Whereas early Tudor historians, notably John Rastell in his *Pastyme of People*, thought of history as morally sound recreation, by the later years of Queen Elizabeth I, when the succession problem became acute, historians who delved too deeply into past rebellions found themselves dangerously near to treasonable plots.[13] John Hayward's description of the deposition of Richard II so fascinated the Earl of Essex that Hayward himself fell under suspicion of involvement in treason, and spent some time in the Tower.[14] The experience made him cautious, and his later writings were openly and unmistakeably royalist. He dedicated *The Lives of the III Norman Kings of England, William the First, William the Second and Henry I* to Charles, Prince of Wales, explaining that it had been written at the request of Charles's deceased elder brother Henry. In his dedication he made a traditional plea for the value of history, writing:

> For by diligent perusing the actes of great men, by considering all the circumstances of them, by comparing Counseiles and Meanes with events, a man may seem to have lived in all ages, to have been present at all enterprises, to be more strongly confirmed in Judgement, to have attained a greater experience than the longest life can possibly afford.[15]

The book itself is essentially a narrative based on a mixture of chronicle and legend. It was spiced occasionally with shrewd speculation, as when he reasoned that William must have had some knowledge of Harald Hardrada's intended invasion, and that his long delay at Saint-Valéry should be attributed, not as some said to contrary winds, but to a deliberate delay until King Harold of England had to withdraw to face the invading armies in the north.[16] His judgements on the effects of the conquest were resolutely royalist. He contrasted the rules of succession (as then established) favourably with previous practices, observing that at some times 'he whose sword could cut best was alwaies adjudged to have most right'.[17] A similar view had been expressed by

Gaimar in his condemnation of eighth-century practices; but it is unlikely that Hayward ever saw a manuscript of Gaimar's poem. He had no doubt of the justice of William I's succession, writing that 'he did not settle himself in the chair of sovereignty as one that had reduced all things to the proud power and pleasure of a conqueror, but as an universal successor of former Kings in all the rights and privileges which they did enjoy'. The change of customs was not sudden, but was always made with the approbation of the English. 'So the change was chiefly in the stem and family of the king .... The State still remained the same, the solid body of the State remained still English'.[18] Although this line of reasoning was to be taken up later in constitutional debates, Hayward himself was concerned rather with precepts for a prince than with polemics.

Sometimes prudence, sometimes genuine tolerance, kept most scholars safely away from potentially treasonable subjects in the early years of James I. Samuel Daniel, historian and poet, who like John Hayward in his later life was close to the court, knew where to look for the virtues of royalty, and praised William the Conqueror's magnanimity towards rebels.[19] Daniel's humane tolerance looked for positive values in the heritage of the past, however stormy. In his *Defence of Ryme* he argued that it must be

> a touch of arrogant ignorance, to hold this or that nation Barbarous, these or those times grosse, considering how this manifold creature man, wheresoever hee stand in the world, hath alwayes some disposition of worth, intertaines the order of societie, affects that which is most in use, and is eminent in some one thing or other that fits his humour and the times .... The *Gothes, Vandales* and *Langobards*, whose coming downe like an inundation overwhelmed, as they say, all the glory of learning in *Europe,* have yet left us still their lawes and customes, as the originalls of most of the provincial constitutions of Christendome.

He urged his readers to go no further, 'but looke upon the wonderfull Architecture of this state of *England,* and see whether they were deformed times, that could give it such a forme'.[20]

Many antiquaries and scholars of the period – who included the country gentry investigating their family origins, royal servants like Lambarde, who worked as Keeper of the Records in the Rolls Chapel or at the Tower of London, and collectors of manuscripts like Cotton – were interested in exploring the wealth of new sources open to them, and, though anxious to understand the institutions of their country, had no wish to become involved in political wrangles. This spirit was behind the first attempt to found a Society of Antiquaries in London about 1586.[21] Sir Henry Spelman, writing in the next century, described their enterprise:

> At this auspicious period, a set of gentlemen of great abilities, many of them students in the inns of court, applied themselves to the study of the antiquities and history of this kingdom, a taste at that time very prevalent, wisely foreseeing that without a perfect knowledge of these requisites, a thorough understanding of the laws of their native country could not be attained.[22]

Members were expected to attend and to give their opinions on such subjects as 'The antiquity of arms in England', 'The antiquity of Ceremonies used at Funerals', 'Sterling Money', or 'The Etymology, Dignity, and Antiquity of Dukes in England'.[23] These were specific, concrete subjects, and the members seldom ventured into speculation on abstract questions like ecclesiastical authority or freedom of conscience. Queen Elizabeth had no quarrel with it; but her successor, James I, suspected that such assemblies of gentlemen might conceal the operations of 'a treasonable cabal', and its meetings were discontinued. Although it was restored briefly between 1614 and 1617 through the efforts of Sir Henry Spelman and other scholars, who insisted on a rule 'that we should neither meddle with matters of State nor Religion', James decided on its suppression.[24]

King James was not entirely unjustified in his misgivings. During the middle years of the seventeenth century serious scholarship was beginning to influence the thinking of reformers and revolutionaries in unexpected ways. The antiquaries like Cotton, always ready to lend the manuscripts in his library to others, brought new material into the historical debate. Specialists in Anglo-Saxon, concerned with philology and early literature, awakened an interest in early English culture that provided a new angle on the Norman Conquest. The learned lawyers, with their knowledge of past precedents and earlier litigation, were nearer to the interface of learning and politics.[25] Nevertheless the legal interpretations of judges such as Sir Matthew Hale were not in themselves contaminated by politics. During the civil war period Hale was prepared to appear in cases against the government, and insisted when challenged, 'I am pleading in defence of the laws which you are bound to maintain. I am doing justice to my client, and am not to be intimidated'.[26] He was so widely respected that after the Restoration Charles II employed him in disputes between landlords and their tenants, and in 1671 he was promoted lord chief justice of England.

Hale's more academic discussion of the Norman Conquest in his *History of the Common Law of England* showed an honest attempt to find the truth in the sources available, some of which unfortunately still needed critical assessment by a new generation of scholars. William I's attaining the crown, he argued, was often called the Conquest of England, 'yet in truth it was not such a Conquest as did or could alter the laws of this kingdom, or impose upon the people by right of battle'.[27] Even in such a conquest, he maintained, the victor was not secure until he had obtained some consent or acceptance by the conquered people.[28] The second kind of conquest was when the conqueror had 'a real right or a formal pretence or claim thereto; he then secured only the rights that his predecessor had enjoyed. William's Conquest was of this kind'.[29] Wrongly believing, like most of his contemporaries, that the dubious post-conquest collections known as the *Laws of King William* and the *Laws of Edward the Confessor* were authentic, he claimed that King William 'enforced them by his own authority and the assent of parliament, at the request of the English' and that he added some new laws relating to military tenures.[30] In spite of flaws and anachronisms in his argument, Hale correctly stated William's claim to be the rightful successor of King Edward and the preserver of his laws. He added, however, that 'it is very probable that after the victory, the Norman nobility and soldiers were scattered through the whole kingdom and mingled with the English; which might possibly introduce some of the Norman laws and customs insensibly into the kingdom'.[31]

Historical investigation arising from legal cases drew practical lawyers, particularly those with an interest in language, into the main controversies about the Norman Conquest. These men were concerned with the practical burdens of a form of tenure which many believed had been introduced by the Normans, and with the question of a supposed 'ancient constitution' and its relation to the authority of law and parliament. Sir Henry Spelman's work was to have a lasting influence on the first question. A lawyer with a keen interest in language, he compiled a *Glossary* in which he defined (tenurial) *feuds* and stated that they had been introduced by the Normans.[32] This view was soon challenged in the law courts. In a 1639 case on defective titles, argued by the Judges of all Ireland, it had been decided 'that Feuds were in use before the Norman Conquest'. Various 'laws and charters' of the Saxon kings were produced, and in the proceedings Spelman's view was rejected. Spelman's reasoned reply, in his treatise on *The Original Growth, Propagation and Condition of Feuds and Tenures by Knight-Service in England* (published posthumously in *Reliquiae Spelmanniae*) argued persuasively against this view.[33] The term *feud*, he pointed out, could be used in two different ways. There was a general definition 'which may be of a temporary nature and not carry Wardship, Marriage and Relief', and also a narrower definition. In this narrower sense, he argued, 'A feud is a right which the vassal hath in land, or some immovable thing of his Lord's, to use the same and take the profits thereof hereditarily: rendering unto his Lord such feudal duties and services as belong to military tenures, the meer propriety of the soil always remaining with the Lord'. He concluded:

> It was neither my words nor my meaning to say that he [William] first brought in either Feuds or Military Service in a general sense, but that he brought in the Servitudes and Grievances of Feuds, viz. Wardships, Marriage and such like, which, to this day were never known to other Nations that are governed by the Feudal Law.[34]

One immediate practical outcome of this debate was the so-called 'abolition of feudal tenures' by the Long Parliament (an abolition which in fact was much more limited in scope than the title suggests).[35] The theoretical, historical controversy, however, had a very long life ahead of it. For over three centuries, few later writers on medieval constitutional history could avoid discussion of 'feudal' obligations, and they were central in any consideration of the effects of the Norman Conquest. Writing in 1939, David Douglas considered that Spelman's *Feuds and Tenures by Knight-Service* 'anticipated much of the most recent work which has been done on English feudal origins'.[36] Some more recent historical investigation has, however, taken a different turn.[37]

Politically more dangerous was the question of the effect that the Norman Conquest might have had on the supposed ancient constitution of the kingdom.[38] This involved lawyers, parliamentarians and pamphleteers, some of them serious scholars, others carried away by popular feeling and ideology. Some parliamentarians argued that this ancient constitution had existed from time immemorial; the most radical, such as the Levellers, believed that it had been subverted by the Normans. Some, who claimed that ancient rights had been embodied in the witan of the Anglo-Saxon kings, demanded similar liberties for the parliaments they imagined had been founded very shortly after the Conquest. Potentially revolutionary, this interpretation of history could be accepted by royalists no less than by parliamentarians, though it was bound to be challenged by the best-informed scholars of any party.

Prynne, the indefatigable pamphleteer whose writings brought him to the pillory and the Tower on more than one occasion, refused to allow history as he found it in the ancient records to be subverted, no matter what it proved. While defending parliament's cause during the war period and the Commonwealth, he insisted that the commons had not been a necessary element in the earliest 'parlements'.[39] His work on the records in the Tower began during the Commonwealth, and he showed that no writs summoning representatives of the commons could be found before the reign of Henry III. After the Restoration his integrity was so respected that he was appointed Keeper of the Records of the Tower. It was he who insisted that the writs for Charles II's first parliament must be issued in the traditional form, in the king's name. His greatest contribution towards steering parliamentary history away from wild speculation was his *Brief Register of Parliamentary Writs*. A massive set of four volumes of over two thousand pages (which belied the 'brief' in its title), it was published between 1658 and 1664. His work has been summarised by Pocock as 'a critical and sophisticated variant of that common-law thought which took the institutions of the present day and sought for their origins in the remote past'.[40]

The political controversies of the civil war period put a stamp on the debates of historians about the Norman Conquest that was to prove enduring. This was the myth of the 'Norman yoke'.[41] Medieval historians, including Orderic Vitalis, who used the phrase, can never have imagined the way in which it was later to be enlarged into a myth.[42] As analysed by Christopher Hill, the myth maintained that the Anglo-Saxons had lived as free and equal citizens before the Norman Conquest, and had governed themselves through representative institutions. The assertion of original Saxon rights could be made by reformers of all kinds, whether they were radical social and political reformers who demanded the restoration of lost rights, or moderates who believed in a continuity of legal tradition that had survived the conquest and could be the basis of reform. The crux was in the interpretation of the nature of William's conquest, already familiar to earlier historians. The change lay in the view of the radicals that considered the conquest to be a revolutionary introduction of a new system, which within a century began to be called 'feudalism'. A belief in the wholesale importation of Norman customs or institutions was to have a lasting and baleful influence on romantic literary views of the past in the nineteenth century, and even on the work of serious academic historians in the twentieth.[43]

Notes

1 Richard Britnell, *The Closing of the Middle Ages? 1471–1529* (Oxford, 1997), pp. 248–50.

2 *Holinshed's Chronicles*, 2 vols (London, 1807–8; repr. New York, 1965), 1, p. 764 (hereafter *Holinshed*). 'Ralph Holinshed's Cronycle' was published in two volumes in 1578; Holinshed was assisted in the work by William Harrison and Richard Stonyhurst; a new, revised edition supervised by John Hooker appeared in 1587. See May McKisack, *Medieval History in the Tudor Age* (Oxford, 1971), p. 116.

3 D. Hay, *Polidore Vergil: Renaissance Historian and Man of Letters* (Oxford, 1952); *Polydore Vergil's English History*, ed. H. Ellis, 2 vols, Camden Society, 1st ser., (London, 1844, 1846), 1, pp. 105–6; McKisack, *Tudor Age*, pp. 99–101.

4 J. A. Guy, *The Public Career of Sir Thomas More* (Brighton, 1980), pp. 100–2, 132–3, 144.

5 McKisack, *Tudor Age*, pp. 114–15.

6 *Holinshed*, 2, p. 72.

7 Thomas Starkey, *A Dialogue between Reginald Pole and Thomas Lupset*, ed. K. M. Burton (London, 1948), pp. 117, 174–5; C. Hill, *Puritanism and*

Revolution (London, 1958), pp. 59–60.

8 McKisack, *Tudor Age*, pp. 170–3, citing William Warren, *Albion's England* (1602), p. 113.

9 McKisack, *Tudor Age*, p. 170.

10 See above, p. 16.

11 H. S. Bennett, *English Books and Readers 1475 to 1557*, 2nd edn (Cambridge, 1969), p. xiii.

12 J. H. Round, *Family Origins* (London, 1930), p. 5.

13 D. C. Douglas, *English Scholars* (London, 1939, repr. 1951), p. 120.

14 Sidney Lee, 'Sir John Hayward', in *Dictionary of National Biography*, 25, pp. 311–13.

15 John Hayward, *The Lives of the III Norman Kings of England, William the First, William the Second and Henry I* (London, 1612), Preface.

16 *Ibid.*, pp. 52–4.

17 *Ibid.*, pp. 42–3.

18 *Ibid.*, pp. 123–4.

19 Samuel Daniel, *The First Part of the History of England* (London, 1612), p. 146.

20 Samuel Daniel, *Poems and a Defence of Rhyme*, ed. A. C. Sprague (Cambridge, Massachusetts, 1930), pp. 140, 145–6.

21 McKisack, *Tudor Age*, p. 75.

22 Sir Henry Spelman, 'Original of the Four Terms', in *Reliquiae Spelmanniae* (Oxford, 1698), pp. 69–70.

23 McKisack, *Tudor Age*, pp. 156–7.

24 Douglas, *English Scholars*, pp. 105–6; M. M. Condon and E. M. Hallam, 'Government printing of the Public Records in the eighteenth century', *Journal of the Society of Archivists* 7 (1984), pp. 348–88, at p. 374.

25 Douglas, *English Scholars*, p. 106.

26 Matthew Hale, *The History of the Common Law*, 5th edn (London, 1794), 1, p. ii.

27 *Ibid.*, 1, p. 147.

28 *Ibid.*, 1, p. 150.

29 *Ibid.*, 1, pp. 164–5.

30 *Ibid.*, 1, p. 7.

31 *Ibid.*, 1, p. 185.

32 Henry Spelman, *Glossarium* (London, 1626), pp. 255–63; (repr. London, 1687), pp. 216–21.

33 *Reliquiae Spelmanniæ*, pp. 1–2.

34 *Ibid.*, p. 46.

35 Susan Reynolds, *Fiefs and Vassals* (Oxford, 1994), p. 7, citing *Statutes of the Realm*, v. 260 (12 Chas. II c. 24, cl. 10).

36 D. C. Douglas, *The Norman Conquest and the British Historians* (David Murray Foundation Lecture, Glasgow, 1946).

37 See below, pp. 79–83.

38 See J. G. A. Pocock, *The Ancient Constitution and the Feudal Law: A Study of English Historical Thought in the Seventeenth Century* (Cambridge, 1957, 2nd edn, 1987); C. Hill, 'The Norman Yoke', in *Puritanism and Revolution* (London, 1958); R. C. Richardson, *The Debate on the English Revolution*

3rd edn (Manchester, 1998), p. 15.
39 Pocock, *Ancient Constitution*, pp. 156–62.
40 *Ibid.*, p. 161.
41 Asa Briggs, *Saxons, Normans and Victorians* (St Leonards-on-Sea, Sussex, 1966), pp. 5–7.
42 *The Ecclesiastical History of Orderic Vitalis*, ed. M. Chibnall, 6 vols, OMT (Oxford, 1969–80), 2, p. 202.
43 See below, Ch. 4.

3

New approaches:
scholars and politicians

Gradually, after the Restoration of Charles II in 1660, controversies about past history moved into calmer waters, though, as R. C. Richardson pointed out, 'the connections between politics and history were far too strong to allow Civil War studies to lapse into a mere academic debate'.[1] The same is true to a much lesser extent of the debate on the Norman Conquest. As long as conspiracies – and rumours of conspiracies – threatened a renewal of civil war, historical speculation could still be dangerous to a man's reputation, even if scholarship was slowly gaining ground against passion. A contrast between James I's anxious suppression of the nascent Society of Antiquaries was provided by Charles II's patronage of the Royal Society, founded in 1662 'for improving natural knowledge'. A private society incorporated by charter, it had a wide membership on the model of continental academies.[2] It brought together men distinguished in various disciplines – historical, archaeological and antiquarian, no less than scientific – and included patrons and dilettanti as well as practitioners. Richard Ollard, the biographer of Samuel Pepys (an early Fellow of the Royal Society), pointed out, in describing the political intrigues that led to Pepys's brief incarceration in the Tower in 1679, that friends with valuable connections helped him. He had contacts through John Evelyn and the Royal Society 'with the great international world of learning and the arts, a passport sometimes more valuable in highly civilised countries than those issued by politicians'.[3] Serious study and international friendships provided new material for debates about the past.

One scholar, singled out by Douglas for the importance of his contribution to the study of the Norman Conquest was Robert Brady, a man of many parts.[4] Trained as a doctor of medicine, he became in 1660 Master of Caius College, Cambridge, as well as Professor of Medicine. He was also physician-in-ordinary to both Charles II and James II, represented his university in the parliaments of both kings, and was appointed Keeper of the Records of the Tower. His principal historical work, the *Complete History of England*, addressed to King James II, showed that in spite of his many interests and responsibilities, he was no dilettante. The list of authorities used by him includes (in addition to more than two dozen chroniclers) Domesday Book, the Patent, Close, and Charter Rolls, and some monastic cartularies. He used his sources critically; his denunciation, in the Preface to his *History*, of the uncritical writers who had gone on copying superficial accounts was based on his own studies.[5] In reply to 'those who cry up the Liberties and Freedom of the ordinary people under the Saxon kings to such a Degree as makes them all Petty Princes, or at least Sharers in Government', he cited numerous passages from Domesday Book to show how greatly the condition of smallholders varied before 1066. With only a little exaggeration and misrepresentation, he complained that, though Coke, Selden, Prynne and others

> write of nothing but the brave feats of the English appearing for their birthrights, and the great privileges they had formerly enjoyed, nobody knows, nor can tell, when or where, when in very Deed they were not English, but incorrigible Norman Rebels against their own Norman Prince, from whom they or their ancestors had received so many and so great benefits and favours.[6]

His work is particularly distinguished by the abundance of citations from records it contains, and for his critical approach to sources others had taken for granted. The 'so-called laws of King Edward', he claimed, were 'an incoherent farce and mixture, and a heap of nonsense'. Norman words in them showed that they were put together after the conquest.[7] Knowing how valuable Domesday Book had been for his own studies, he pleaded that it should be made generally accessible. At that time, though the value of Domesday Book was recognised, those who had not Brady's own easy access as Keeper of the Records in the Tower had to pay a fee of six shillings and eightpence to use it, with an additional fourpence for every line transcribed and six pence for the paper on which to copy it.[8] Brady's transcripts were fuller than those of any other scholar at that time; and though his wish for an edition of Domesday Book was not fulfilled for nearly a century, other learned men authorised to work in the public records gradually made more of those records available in print.

Moreover some scholars working in the universities of Oxford and Cambridge continued to make a contribution to medieval studies. In particular, the advance of Anglo-Saxon studies prepared the way for a closer examination of the changes that might have been introduced by the Norman Conquest. In 1659 William Somner, the first holder of a lectureship in Old English established at Cambridge by Henry Spelman, produced his *Dictionarium Saxonico-Latino-Anglicum*, the first comprehensive Anglo-Saxon dictionary to be published.[9] It was the indispensible tool for serious research in the Anglo-Saxon chronicles and laws, and set a new standard of impartial criticism. George Hickes, the scholarly bishop of Worcester, who was proscribed and persecuted as one of the non-jurors, carried on his research resolutely and impartially even when he was in hiding.[10] His greatest achievements were philological; the Norman Conquest came into his studies because of the language. Writing to one of his students he stated, 'I am now in the chapter *De Dialectico Normannico-Saxonico*, which furnishes me with pleasant theories about the alteration of the Saxon upon the Norman Conquest. This makes me resolve to give the world a specimen of the many *Gallica* out of Domesday Book and the red book of the Chequer'.[11] The book was warmly praised by Mabillon.[12] By showing that the Old English language should not be studied in isolation apart from Nordic languages, Hickes brought a Scandinavian element into the interpretation of the causes and consequences of the Norman Conquest.[13]

At the same time the publication of the official records, which may be said to have been initiated by Prynne and Brady as Keepers of the Records, began to be tackled a little more systematically. Sorting and printing the vast accumulation of records was a formidable task, which was first attempted by two industrious and dedicated holders of the office of historiographer royal. They devoted themselves not merely to transcribing documents, but to studying them critically and scientifically. Previous holders of the office, even when learned men, had not considered publishing the records to be one of their duties; indeed Thomas Rymer, appointed in 1693, wrote critically of his predecessors:

> You are not to expect truth from an historiographer royal; it may drop from their pen by chance, but the general herd understand not their business; they fill in with story, accidental, incoherent, without end or side, and never know the *government* or *policy* of what they write. Even the Records themselves are not always accurately worded.[14]

Rymer's task was to make available the treaties and documents concerned with foreign relations. Such transactions had once been regarded as secret, but a greater openness had crept in during the civil wars as a result of the need to canvas public opinion, and the emergence of a new type of journalism. In Germany Leibnitz was in the process of publishing diplomatic documents, primarily as material for practical statesmen, but with the subsidiary intention of helping students of history.[15] Rymer corresponded with Leibnitz and learnt much from him. Between 1704 and 1713, when he died, Rymer produced fifteen massive folio volumes of his *Foedera*, which were published by the Treasury. Rymer's methods came in for criticism later; T. D. Hardy said that 'he could be unsystematic in his selection and cavalier in his exercise of editorial judgement'. But the documents were carefully copied from the best exemplars Rymer could find; and the task was too great for a single scholar.[16]

Thomas Madox, his successor in office as historiographer royal, had previously been working for some time among the Public Records in the Tower and various other government offices, and in 1702 had produced his *Formulare Anglicanum*, compiled from the 'vast collection of Ancient Original Charters' in the Repository of the Court of Augmentations.[17] In the introduction to almost eight hundred charters he laid down for the first time the principles to be applied in editing such texts.[18] Charters, he insisted, were the fundamental sources of feudal history. Whenever possible he worked from original documents, not cartulary copies, and printed every word, including the names of witnesses, giving close attention to handwriting and formulae. In this he followed the eminent French scholar and monk, Jean

Mabillon, whose *De re diplomatica* had for the first time set out the rules to be followed in editing documents and distinguishing authentic from forged charters.[19] Mabillon stated the need to examine the materials used, the signature, the grammar and orthography, the mode of address, the plausibility of the dating, and the intrinsic consistency of the whole document. His work laid the foundation for the science of diplomatic, which Madox helped to bring to England.

Madox's second great work was the *History and Antiquities of the Exchequer from the Norman Conquest to the end of the reign of King Edward II*. Among the documents he printed was Richard fitz Nigel's *Dialogue of the Exchequer*, which described the workings of the Exchequer in the reign of Henry II.[20] This had been known in transcript to scholars including Coke, Spelman, Lambarde and Twysden, but had never before been critically edited and published with a convincing dating and attribution. Earlier attributions had mostly been, improbably, to Gervase of Tilbury.[21] While neither Madox nor Rymer dealt specifically with the effects of the Norman Conquest, their work was of substantial value to future scholars investigating the changes of the eleventh and twelfth centuries. As Madox set out in his Preface to the *Formulare Anglicanum*:

> I think one may say in general that for want of a close Inspection and Use of the Ancient Records and Memoirs of this Kingdom, many crude and precarious Things have been advanced concerning our Old Laws and Constitutions: Men having been tempted, as it seems, to frame hypotheses concerning the Ancient State of Things from either Modern or Present Appearances.[22]

In his opinion, proper understanding of the history of a country depended upon a thorough study of its records,

> For I think it is to be wished, that the Histories of a Countrey so well furnished with Records and Manuscripts as Ours is, should be grounded throughout (as far as is practicable) on proper Vouchers. And for my part, I cannot look upon the *History of England* to be compleatly written, till it shall come to be written after that manner.[23]

Madox and Rymer were among the scholars who helped to set in motion the movement for making available the public records of the nation. Domesday Book had a high priority. Humphrey Wanley, Lord Harley's learned librarian and one of the founders of the Society of Antiquaries as restored in 1707, stressed its importance. Unfortunately, printing it presented many problems. A special type was needed to attempt to reproduce the abbreviations, and a reliable transcriber had to be found. Finally, in 1768, Abraham Farley, a deputy chamberlain of the Exchequer who had been working on Domesday Book for more than twenty-five years, was asked to superintend its printing. By 1783 two volumes, containing the text of Domesday and Little Domesday, were ready. Printed by and for Parliament, they were intended at first for official reference and were not for sale. Copies were sent to chosen institutions, including the universities of Oxford and Cambridge, and at first they circulated very slowly. But it was a beginning of very high quality; Farley's work has stood the test of time.[24] From 1800 a series of record commissions were set up with the express aim of making the records available in print; and in 1816 two further volumes were added to provide an index and an edition of the Exeter Domesday and other 'Domesday satellites'.[25] It should not be forgotten that, at a time when history was not very highly rated by many of the intelligentsia, a valuable official contribution to historical study was slowly and hesitantly being made. Much of the general historical writing of the period turned aside into philosophy and politics. Medieval English history tended to be either neglected or accorded a minor place as a diversion in gentlemanly culture, and a contribution to table-talk.

After the 1688 Revolution, the reference to the Laws of Edward the Confessor was omitted from the coronation oath.[26] The omission indicated a change in historical and political thinking. The common-law tradition, with its stress on immemorial custom, remained a strong undercurrent; but ideas on an ancient constitution were being replaced by a theory of contract. John Locke's views were among the more extreme; he believed that law was derived from the will of every individual to secure his natural rights. Will to him was grounded in 'principles of nature and reason which lie outside history altogether'.[27] There was no place for the Norman Conquest in such a philosophy. The Scots philosopher, David Hume (1711–76) allowed more value to history in the course of reasoning, even if his conclusions had something in common with those of Locke. He considered that history had a place in 'an empirical science of man'; and he was more prepared than some of his contemporaries to include the Middle Ages in his *History of Great Britain*.[28] Indeed Duncan Forbes has commented that the medieval section, usually unread, 'is in many ways a remarkable achievement'.[29]

Yet even Hume introduced the conquest only to dismiss it. He adopted the common contemporary view that contrasted 'feudalism' with 'the nation', and wrote:

> The vast fabric of feudal subordination became quite solid and comprehensive; it formed everywhere an essential part of the political constitution; and the Norman and other barons who followed the fortunes of William were so accustomed to it that they could scarcely form an idea of any other species of civil government.[30]

He added, however, that the northern nations 'had no idea that any man trained up to honour and inured to arms was ever to be governed without his own consent by the absolute will of another'. The first kings of the Normans, he claimed,

> were generals of a conquering army, which was obliged to continue in a military posture, and to maintain great subordination under their leader, in order to secure themselves from the revolt of the numerous natives .... But though this circumstance supported the authority of William and his immediate successors, it was lost as soon as the Norman barons began to incorporate with the nation.[31]

This virtually reduced the conquest to a hiccup in the growth of the nation. He complained particularly of the 'feudal law' which introduced primogeniture, so producing and maintaining an unequal division of private property.[32] Social evils had resulted from the conquest, but he had no interest in the older question of what kind of a conquest it had been, or in the more recent question of the ancient constitution.

Many historians treated the Norman Conquest together with the whole of the Middle Ages much more cavalierly. Bolingbroke considered that much of the material collected by antiquaries was learned lumber not worth the waste of time, and that many people read history simply for amusement or to shine in conversation.[33] While allowing that history ought to be studied by

serious men as a training in public and private virtues, he maintained that not all periods of history were worthy of the same
attention. Certain eras were of greater importance. Affairs, he
asserted, are closely linked together, but 'the whole connection
diminishes as the chain lengthens, till at last it seems to be
broken'. A new system gave rise to new interests; some analogy
between eras might exist, 'but it will soon become an object of
mere curiosity, not of profitable inquiry'. In his opinion a new
system of causes and effects began with each era:

> To be entirely ignorant about the ages which precede this era would
> be shameful .... But to be learned about them is a ridiculous affecta-
> tion in any man who means to be useful to this present era. Down to
> this era let us read history; from this era, and down to our own time,
> let us study it.[34]

He considered that 'the present era' began towards the end of the
fifteenth century. In such an interpretation there was little room
for the Norman Conquest.

The view expressed by Bolingbroke – that only a few periods
of history deserved serious study was prevalent among writers in the
later eighteenth century. Voltaire thought that only four periods
deserved the attention of persons of taste: the age of Pericles, the
epoch of Augustuse, the Italian renaissance, and the reign of Louis
XIV.[35] Many of the intelligentsia used history as material for table-
talk. Even Samuel Johnson was prepared to pronounce (in the
presence of Gibbon) that 'We must consider how very little real
history there is; I mean real authentick history. That certain Kings
reigned and certain battles were fought we can depend upon as true;
but all the colouring, all the philosophy of history is conjecture'.[36]
Johnson's view, expressed on another occasion, was typical of many
more than those who belonged to his circle:

> Great abilities are not requisite for an Historian; for in historical
> composition all the greatest powers of the human mind are quies-
> cent. He has facts ready to his hand: so there is no exercise of
> invention. Imagination is not required in any high degree; only
> about as much as is used in the lower kinds of poetry. Some penetra-
> tion, accuracy and colouring, will fit a man for the task if he can give
> the application which is necessary.[37]

Legal studies had much less direct influence than formerly on those involved in politics. The Inns of Court were ceasing to be the 'third university'; by about 1720 most politicians studied in Oxford or Cambridge, away from the common-law training. Among the politically active, the most prevalent view of the past (not in fact confined to Whigs) was what came to be described as the 'Whig interpretation of history'. This triumphed most completely later, in the work of Macaulay. Herbert Butterfield has defined it as 'the tendency in many historians to write on the side of Protestants and Whigs, to praise revolutions provided they have been successful, to emphasize certain principles of progress in the past and to produce a story which is the ratification if not the glorification of the present'.[38] Macaulay's statement that 'the history of our country during the last hundred and sixty years is eminently the history of physical, of moral, and of intellectual improvement' was a typical expression of the kind of historical complacency that had been nurtured during the eighteenth century.[39]

A legal approach to politics survived, however in writers on legal history. Martin Wright, who wrote an *Introduction to the Law of Tenures* in 1730, tackled the question of whether 'military feuds' were brought into England by the Conqueror, and he came down on the side of Spelman and Hale that they were an innovation, and against Selden and Nathaniel Bacon, who considered them to have been common among the Saxons.[40] He is unusual in looking closely at particular historical events that seemed to him to mark a significant change. In particular, he cites the homage done to William the Conqueror at London and Salisbury some twenty years after the conquest, and argues that, since this was done about the time that Domesday Book was finished, 'we may suppose that that Survey was taken upon, or soon after, our Ancestors' Consent to Tenures, in order to discover the quantity of every man's Fee, and to fix his homage'.[41] He claimed that

> the establishment of Tenures was an extraordinary Alteration, because it originally and immediately defeated all Supposition or Possibility of Propriety in any Person other than the King. It became a fundamental necessary Maxim, Principle or Fiction of our English Law of Tenures, that the King is universal Lord of his whole Territories, and that no Man doth, or can possess any Part thereof, or Lands therein, but as either mediately or immediately derived from him.[42]

It was important to him that this 'Principle of Tenures' was a fiction, and that William did not hold all the lands of England in demesne; and he enlarged upon the legal processes by which William distributed the land, citing the great trials at Penenden and elsewhere. Following the contemporary interpretation that saw the council as a forerunner of parliament, he emphasised the implicit consent of the *commune consilium*.[43] He ended with a disavowal of any claim to finality,

> I now submit the Whole of this Essay to the further Enquiry and Correction of the Reader; adverting him only, that as the Attempt is new and the Subject much obscured by Time, and Want of Contemporary Lights to clear it, the Author begs Allowance for Mistakes, and that the Reader will better inform him.[44]

When Blackstone discussed feudal tenures in his *Commentaries*, he adopted Martin Wright's general argument. He proposed that 'the feudal law' was apparently not universally established in England till the reign of William the Norman,

> though something similar was in use among the Saxons .... This introduction however of the feudal tenures into England, by King William, does not seem to have been immediately after the conquest, nor by the mere arbitrary will and power of the conqueror; but to have been gradually established by the Norman barons, and others, in such forfeited lands as they received from the gift of the conqueror, and afterwards universally consented to by the great council of the nation long after his title was established.[45]

It was 'not so much imposed as freely adopted'; and, though severe dues and services were imposed, a movement against them built up through Magna Carta and other charters to the 'restoration of the ancient constitution'.[46] This was a neat adaptation of legal history to the prevailing mood of freedom and consent to government, and was compatible with (though different from) David Hume's view. One of Wright's observations, picked up by Blackstone, was not, however, much noticed until the late twentieth century, when J. C. Holt reviewed the suggestion of a possible connection between the 'Salisbury oaths' and the making of Domesday Book.[47]

Notes

1 R. C. Richardson, *The Debate on the English Revolution*, 3rd edn (Manchester, 1998), p. 42.
2 Marie Boas Hall, *All Scientists Now* (Cambridge, 1984), pp. ix–x.
3 Richard Ollard, *Pepys, A Biography* (London, 1974; pbk edn 1993), p. 284.
4 D. C. Douglas, *English Scholars* (London, 2nd edn, 1951), p. 125.
5 Robert Brady, *A Complete History of England* (London, 1685), General Preface.
6 *Ibid.*, Letter to the Reader.
7 *Ibid.*, p. xxx.
8 M. M. Condon and E. M. Hallam, 'Government printing of the Public Records in the eighteenth century', *Journal of the Society of Archivists*, 7 (1984), pp. 348–88, at p. 373.
9 Douglas, *English Scholars*, pp. 55–6.
10 *Ibid.*, pp. 82–97.
11 *Ibid.*, p. 85.
12 See above, p. 45.
13 Earlier writers from William of Poitiers onwards had concentrated on Norman influences; see above, pp. 9–10, for the official version of the Norman case, based on Norman records.
14 T. D. Hardy, *Syllabus ... of the Documents contained in the Collection known as Rymer's 'Foedera'* (London, 1869–85), 1, p. xxii; cf. F. W. Maitland, *Collected Papers*, 3 vols, ed. H. A. L. Fisher (Cambridge, 1911), 3, p. 407, 'The spirit which animated Thomas Madox was not at home in academic circles. Most of the regius professors wrote nothing'.
15 Douglas, *English Scholars*, p. 226.
16 Condon and Hallam, 'Government printing', pp. 349–59.
17 Douglas, *English Scholars*, p. 235.
18 T. Madox, *Formulare Anglicanum* (London, 1702), Preface, sect. vi.
19 David Knowles, 'Jean Mabillon', in his *The Historian and Character* (Cambridge, 1963), pp. 213–39, at pp. 222–3.
20 Richard fitz Nigel, *Dialogus de Scaccario*, ed. Charles Johnson, corr. F. E. L. Carter and D. E. Greenway, OMT (Oxford, 1983).
21 *Dialogus*, pp. xiii–xiv.
22 Madox, *Formulare Anglicanum*, Preface.
23 *Ibid.*, p. v.
24 Condon and Hallam, 'Government printing', pp. 374–83; *Domesday Book: seu liber censualis Willelmi primi regis Angliae inter archivos regni in domo capitulari asservatus*, 2 vols (London, printed by J. Nichols, 1783).
25 Condon and Hallam, 'Government printing', pp. 282–3; *Libri censualis, vocati Domesday Book, indices* (London, 1816); *Libri censualis, vocati Domesday Book, additamenta* (London, 1816), the work of Sir Henry Ellis.
26 J. G. A. Pocock, *The Ancient Constitution and the Feudal Law* (Cambridge, 1957; 2nd edn, 1987), pp. 229–30.
27 John Locke, *Two Treatises of Civil Government* (London, 1690), second treatise.
28 David Hume, *The History of Great Britain*, ed. Duncan Forbes (London,

1754; repr. Harmondsworth, Middlesex, 1970), Introduction (by Forbes), p. 9.

29 *Ibid.*, p. 10.

30 David Hume, *The History of England to the Revolution in 1688*, ed. R. W. Kilcup (London, 1754–62; abridged, Chicago and London, 1975), p. 10.

31 *Ibid.*, p. 15.

32 *Ibid.*, p. 38.

33 *The Works of Lord Bolingbroke*, 4 vols (London, 1844; repr. 1967), 2, pp. 173–4.

34 *Ibid.*, pp. 238–9.

35 Douglas, *English Scholars*, p. 278.

36 James Boswell, *The Life of Samuel Johnson*, 2 vols in 1, Everyman edn (London, Melbourne and Toronto, 1978), 1, p. 559.

37 *Ibid.*, p. 263.

38 H. Butterfield, *The Whig Interpretation of History* (London, 1931), p. 9.

39 T. B. Macaulay, *History of England* (London, 1852), pp. 14, 23–4, cited in Richardson, *English Revolution*, p. 72.

40 Martin Wright, *An Introduction to the Law of Tenures*, printed by E. R. Nutt and R. Gosling in the Savoy (London, 1730), pp. 5–50.

41 *Ibid.*, pp. 52–4.

42 *Ibid.*, pp. 58–9.

43 *Ibid.*, pp. 59–62.

44 *Ibid.*, pp. 221–2.

45 William Blackstone, *Commentaries on the Laws of England*, 4 vols (Oxford, 1770), 2, p. 48.

46 *Ibid.*, 2, pp. 50–2.

47 See below, pp. 83–4.

4

The nineteenth century: amateurs and professionals

The social and democratic movements that shook Europe after the French Revolution, the upheavals of the Industrial Revolution, and the growth of a strong spirit of nationalism, together with the philosophy of Marxism, transformed both literature and history. Individual freedom was championed by poets and novelists; an imaginary golden age of freedom in the distant past left its mark on history. The Saxons were seen as heroes fighting for personal freedom and self-government against the tyranny of Norman 'feudalism'. Added to this, Karl Marx built a feudal, pre-capital system into his philosophy of history.[1] Once again the Norman Conquest was central, with some strange consequences for historical writing.

At a time when the romantic view of the past was being suggested in literature, Walter Scott provided a link with history through his novels set in the Middle Ages. He justified his method in the Introduction to *Ivanhoe*, insisting that he was not polluting history by mingling it with fiction. In defence of his imputation of motives to his characters, he insisted that 'the passions, the sources from which these must spring in all their modifications, are generally the same in all ranks and conditions, all countries and ages' – a view that was more likely in the long run to prove acceptable to poets than to historians and anthropologists.[2] Walter Scott gave a new emotional appeal to the case for the down-trodden Saxons by linking it with the many-faceted legends about Robin Hood. As J. C. Holt pointed out,

> So far no one had suggested that he [Robin] stood for the oppressed Anglo-Saxon, the genuine Englishman, struggling against the

Norman oppressor. That role was foisted upon him by Sir Walter Scott in *Ivanhoe* in 1819 and by Augustin Thierry in his *Histoire de la conquête de l'Angleterre par les Normands* of 1824. There was nothing to support it .... Scott simply followed the traditional chronology for Robin. The rest was his own romantic inspiration. His historical premise that 'four generations had not sufficed to blend the hostile blood of the Normans and Anglo-Saxons, or to unite, by common language and mutual interests, two hostile races, one of whom felt the elation of triumph, while the other groaned under all the consequences of defeat' was false.[3]

In France, Augustin Thierry was so carried away by this view of the heroic struggle that he compared the position of the English under the Normans to that of the Greeks under the Turks, 'for the special character that the national spirit takes on through suffering under oppression'.[4] Somewhat earlier, Napoleon had linked the Norman Conquest to the triumph of national feeling in a different way. In 1803, when he was planning to invade England, he had the Bayeux Tapestry sent to Paris for an Exhibition, and examined it closely. When the planned invasion was abandoned, he returned the Tapestry to Bayeux, instructing the citizens to 'bring renewed zeal to the task of preserving this fragile relic, which records one of the most memorable deeds of the French nation, and likewise serves as a memorial to the enterprise and courage of our forefathers'.[5]

Benjamin Disraeli, whether or not he was convinced by the distortion of history in *Ivanhoe*, found the myth convenient for his attack on social injustice in England when he published *Sybil, or, The Two Nations* in 1855. The two nations were the rich and the poor; one character, a craftsman who claimed to be of pure Saxon stock, insisted that the history of the conquest of England by the Normans 'must interest all, and all alike, for we are divided between the conquerors and the conquered'.[6] Since the hero of Disraeli's novel was an aristocratic member of parliament, who bridged the division by taking up the cause of the poor and marrying the beautiful 'Saxon', Sybil, he may have intended the book as a blueprint for future Conservative policy. Philippa Levine has suggested that 'Disraeli's Young England derived much of its philosophy directly from that most tenacious of Victorian mythologies, the idealisation of the Middle Ages'.[7]

This idealisation was fostered in the works of other novelists, including Charles Kingsley, author of *Hereward the Wake* and, like Disraeli, also a member of parliament; and George Borrow, who when travelling by train across England averted his eyes from the ruins of a Norman castle, the symbol of Norman tyranny.[8] Thomas Carlyle, after a hasty reading of Jocelyn of Brakelond, provided an idealised picture of medieval rural life in *Past and Present*. Parents gave their children Old English names, such as Alfred, Harold, Egbert, and Ethelwyn. Moreover the increased interest in history at all levels, from the groups who founded local history societies to the most learned Saxonists in the universities and educationalists seeking for ideas on sound methods of education in the distant past, helped for a time to foster the myth of the oppressed and noble Saxons. The myth was equally acceptable to amateurs and professionals, members of parliament and electors. Olive Anderson has argued that, 'In mid nineteenth-century England history was not all things to all men, but there were few men concerned with politics to whom it was not something'.[9] And the romantic reconstruction of the past in novels continued to be a strong influence on history, even after scientific studies, stimulated by Darwin, Huxley and others, began to have an impact on all branches of thought.

From the mid-nineteenth century onwards, mass culture and academic specialisation grew side by side.[10] To many the stability of England in 1848, when so much of Europe was shaken by revolution, was a happy outcome of its past history, and particularly of its strong Saxon roots. New local history societies were founded, more and more people became active members of learned societies, and the government began to take a more positive part in the preservation and publication of both records and chronicles. A new Public Record Office was established in Fetter Lane, London, in 1850, and a series of Historical Manuscripts Commissions tackled, with varying success, the enormous task of preserving and sorting documents in both private and public libraries, so as to make them more widely available. Most notable among the government-inspired enterprises was the launching in 1851 of the *Chronicles and Memorials of Great Britain and Ireland during the Middle Ages* (known as the 'Rolls Series').[11] The volumes, as the prefatory note in each volume states, were to be 'selected for publication under competent editors' authorised by the Master of the Rolls. Although a number of the mostly amateur editors fell short of even the most elementary competence, and one of the best, William Stubbs, had to apply four times before being selected as an editor, the better books in the series have been a mainstay of historical study for over a century. David Knowles, after commenting in a 1960 lecture that 'it was from the beginning an extraordinarily inexpert affair', summed up its sometimes bizarre history by asking,

> Who, among English medievalists of the past seventy years, could have done without it? Who will suggest that, had it never come into being, we should even by 1960 have better editions of all the more significant works? And without all these texts it is difficult to see how the great revolution in academic history, which has sprung primarily from medieval constitutional and institutional history, could ever have taken place. [12]

University history courses began to be established; Oxford had an examination school in modern history in the 1850s, and a separate historical tripos was established in Cambridge in 1873.[13] There were some parallel developments in France, where local antiquarian societies were active. The École des Chartes was established in 1821 to train students in the interpretation of documents. It gave steady support to critical historical studies; though the greatest Norman historian, Léopold Delisle, who happened to be enrolled at the École at the time of the 1848 Revolution, when it was mostly closed, learned more from antiquarian friends at his home in Normandy, and from working on manuscripts of all kinds in the archives and libraries of Paris, than in the lecture rooms of the École.[14] In the USA, historical interests took a somewhat different course. During the middle years of the century 'pictureque history' produced a wildly romantic patchwork from all periods of the Middle Ages, with particular emphasis on the vikings; the academic reaction, when it came, was all the stronger.[15] In England, where the picturesque was more restrained, 'the transition from "literary" to professional history was ... not a break, but a continuum in which, by and large, the demands of professionalism accomodated themselves to the assumptions of "literary" history rather than vice versa'.[16] It was only in the last decades of the nineteenth century that Acton who, as a young man, had admired the romanticists for fostering historical imagination, recognised that they were 'utterly lacking in criticism'.[17]

Earlier in the century some of the most valuable critical work was in Anglo-Saxon studies, which blended in happily with the prevalent romantic myths. John Kemble, a Cambridge graduate who had studied philology in Germany under Jacob Grimm, saw language as the best medium for understanding historical no less than grammatical developments, and helped to revivify Anglo-Saxon studies by editing texts. His *Codex Diplomaticus* (1839–48) was a lasting stimulus to the writing of Anglo-Saxon history; and his two-volume history, *The Saxons in England*, has been called 'the first social history of early England to be based on a sound knowledge of a wide range of Anglo-Saxon sources'.[18] It stated more explicitly Kemble's belief that what was best in English institutions came from Saxon origins, after temporary corruption by Norman tyranny.[19] Benjamin Thorpe's *History of England under the Saxon Kings* was similarly slanted.[20] So in the academic studies of the Norman Conquest that proliferated in the later nineteenth century the Saxonists had a head start.

The widening of university historical teaching received a new impetus with the appointment of William Stubbs (1829–1901) as regius professor of modern history at Oxford in 1866. Although the chair had been established by King George I, most of the previous incumbents had taught little and written less. Stubbs took advantage of the opportunities offered in a more favourable academic climate. His own interest in history had begun in his boyhood, when his father, a Knaresborough solicitor, had trained him to read charters and deeds. After taking an Oxford degree in classics and mathematics, he became a parish priest at Navestock in Essex; and there he employed all his spare time working on medieval records and chronicles, many of which were published in the Rolls Series.[21] Oxford gave him scope for teaching and writing. His greatest work, *The Constitutional History of England* was published in three volumes between 1873 and 1878; it established constitutional history as a distinct subject in the history schools. Remarkable for its substantial learning, its future influence was limited by Stubbs's assumption that English history had been a steady advance towards the establishment of a free, liberal and democratic nation that ought to be a model for others.

He saw continuity and inevitability in the growth of the English constitution. As he wrote in the introduction to the first edition of his *Select Charters*,

> The study of Constitutional History is essentially a tracing of causes and consequences: the examination of a distinct growth from a well-defined germ to full maturity: a growth, the particular direction and shaping of which are due to a diversity of causes, but whose life and developing power lies deep in the very nature of the people. It is not then the collection of a multitude of facts and views, but the piecing of the links of a perfect chain.[22]

The book became prescribed reading in the history faculty and was to keep its importance for decades to come, with results that, however beneficial at first, were later to prove limiting to the study of constitutional history. He was, however, a dedicated and admired teacher, whose friends included the foreign scholars F. Liebermann, R. Pauli and G. Waitz, and the English E. A. Freeman and J. R. Green, as well as the great critic of the work of Freeman, J. H. Round.

The weakest section of his *Constitutional History* was the Anglo-Saxon and early Norman period. This is not altogether surprising, since Stubbs's interest in the work of the German historians was counterbalanced by his almost total ignorance of what the French were doing. Moreover his somewhat teleological view of historical development led him to simplify and exaggerate German influence. 'The English', he wrote 'are a people of German descent in the main constituents of blood, character and language, but most especially in the possession of the elements of primitive German civilisation and the common germs of German institutions'.[23] He put forward as probable a suggestion that 'the polity developed by the German races on British soil is the purest product of their primitive instinct'; and insisted that English common law was based on 'usages anterior to the influx of feudality, that is, on strictly primitive custom'.[24] As for the Norman influence, he relied on a rather sketchy reading of Freeman and Palgrave, and tried to find possible 'founders' of Norman feudalism. His general definition of 'feudalism' as 'the comprehensive idea which includes the whole governmental policy of the French kingdom, which was of distinctly French growth', could scarcely have been vaguer; and his statement that, 'In the form which it has reached at the Norman Conquest, it may be described as a complete organisation of society through the medium of land tenure, in which from the king down to the lowest landowner all are bound together by obligation of service and defence',[25] was to mislead many before being demolished piecemeal by future scholars. Valuable as much of his work undoubtedly was, his contribution to the historiography of the Norman Conquest imposed something of a strait-jacket on historical studies in many universities.

Among his friends were two protagonists who came to represent opposed views on the history of the Norman Conquest: Freeman and Round. Romantic nationalism found its most complete English expression in the historical work of Edward Augustus Freeman (1823–92). His interest in the Norman Conquest began while he was a student at Oxford in 1846, when he wrote an unsuccessful prize essay on 'The effects of the Conquest of England by the Normans'.[26] An indefatigable scholar, with an unrivalled knowledge of medieval chronicles, he finally published his monumental work, *The History of the Norman Conquest of England*, in six volumes in 1867–79. *The Reign of William Rufus*, in two volumes, followed three years later. He consciously set out to appeal to a wide readership of both amateurs and professionals; his avowed aim was stated in a letter of 1867: 'I have to make my text a narrative which I hope may be intelligible to girls and curates, and in an appendix to discuss the evidence for each point in a way which I hope may be satisfactory to Gneist and Stubbs'.[27] Although he was elected regius professor of modern history at Oxford to succeed Stubbs in 1894, he 'made little impact on the Oxford History School'.[28]

Freeman saw English history as a progress towards the triumphant emergence of 'the English nation' with its free parliamentary institutions. His heroes were Earl Godwine and his son Harold, the champions of freedom against the Norman oppressors. Identifying himself with his imagined England, and ignoring the Danish origin of the Godwine family, he wrote of the years after Edward the Confessor became king in 1042: 'The great national reaction under Godwine and Harold made England once more England for a few years'.[29] And he wrote of Edward the

Confessor's reign, when a few of the Normans who had accompanied him had settled in England: 'We have seen Norman adventurers entrenching themselves with English estates, and covering the land with those frowning castles on which our fathers looked as the special badges of wrong and slavery'.[30] In his work Godwine and Harold at times spoke more like nineteenth-century liberal parliamentarians than eleventh-century earls. No wonder he was savagely attacked by Round, and even the courteous Maitland commented to Round, 'he can say funny things at times, and you do right to correct him'.[31] Yet in spite of his faults, his knowledge of the printed chronicle sources for English history was remarkable, and his work had the virtue of seeing that the conquest could not be understood without knowledge of the earlier history of both England and Normandy. His insistence on the continuity of Anglo-Saxon institutions through the period of the Norman Conquest was sufficiently plausible to attract considerable support among later historians, including F. M. Stenton.[32] Indeed, after the onslaught on his historical writing spear-headed by Round had subsided, the solid basis of his work became appreciated by scholars from David Douglas to Ann Williams.[33] Unfortunately the exaggerations of his narrative and the bitterness of Round's attack encouraged the growth of opposed historical camps of Anglo-Saxonists and pro-Normans, and helped to distort some of the historical writing of the twentieth century.

John Horace Round (1854–1928), like some of the seventeenth-century antiquarians, was a man of private means, who came from one of the landed families of Essex. His background and upbringing gave him a strong interest in history and genealogy. Most of his life was spent outside professional academic circles, but as a young man he studied at Oxford, where he attended the lectures of Stubbs at the same time as R. A. L. Poole and T. F. Tout. Stubbs was to him a revered master, and he shared many of his master's views on the purpose and study of history.[34] His own writings were devoted chiefly to the critical examination of documentary sources, particularly charters and royal records from Domesday Book to the Pipe Rolls, and his greatest achievements were in interpreting such records. Like all his English contemporaries, he learned by practical experience and had no formal training in palaeography and diplomatic – a lack which left him somewhat at a disadvantage when he found himself in disagreement with Léopold Delisle.[35]

Unlike Stubbs, Round wrote no narrative history of any kind. The nearest approach to a general history was his *Geoffrey de Mandeville*, published in 1892, the year in which (as Edmund King has pointed out) he himself became a Deputy Lieutenant of the county of Essex, the county of Geoffrey's earldom.[36] In explaining his reasons for producing the book, he expressed his admiration for Stubbs, writing,

> 'The reign of Stephen' in the words of our greatest living historian, 'is one of the most important in our history, as exemplifying the working of causes and principles which had no other opportunity of exhibiting their real tendencies.' To illustrate in detail the working of those principles to which the Bishop of Oxford thus refers is the chief object I have set before myself in these pages.[37]

In this passage Round showed his acceptance of the somewhat deterministic 'cause-and-effect chain' of development described by Stubbs, and more particularly in his view of Stephen's reign as the time in which 'feudal anarchy which had sometimes prevailed abroad but never before in England' first appeared.[38] Round wrote that the charters of Geoffrey de Mandeville would 'form the very backbone' of his work, and that he hoped to break 'a few stones towards the road on which future historians will travel'.[39] His hope was fulfilled, in that many future historians did indeed travel along this road, without realising any more than he did that it might lead them into a maze of controversy and barren speculation. The stones, however, were valuable; for Round's contribution to the critical analysis of charters was substantial. It became unfortunate only when it was combined with his view of the way in which history might be traced back too inflexibly from the known to the unknown, and applied to the interpretation of the effects of the Norman Conquest.

Round's studies of early charters and of the twelfth-century Exchequer records led him gradually to a view of the effects of the Norman Conquest that modified the interpretation of Stubbs and was in direct conflict with that of Freeman. Whereas Freeman had argued against the 'fatal habit' of beginning the study of English history with the Norman Conquest itself,[40] Round insisted that 'our consecutive political history does, in a sense begin with the Norman Conquest' which brought suddenly 'a strong, purposeful monarchy' and the historians ready and able to record its history.[41] He allowed, as he acknowledged Freeman had done, that the conquest began in a sense with the reign of Edward the Confessor, who was brought up in Normandy and took with him the first Norman knights to settle in England. But these knights were merely a hint of what was to come. In the study that was to be his most influential contribution to the debate on the effects of the conquest, 'The introduction of knight service into England', he wrote:

> In approaching the consideration of the institutional changes and modifications of policy resulting from the Norman Conquest, the most conspicuous phenomenon to attract attention is undoubtedly the introduction of what it is convenient to term the feudal system.[42]

Round allowed that completing the change took a little time; but, while rejecting Stubbs's belief that the imposition of quotas of knights on the holders of land took place in the reign of William Rufus, and may have been the work of Ranulf Flambard, he still saw the whole system of *servicia debita* as the Norman importation of a type of military tenure already familiar in Normandy. These conclusions were reached by working backwards towards Domesday Book from the 1166 Inquest into the quotas of service that were recorded in the *Red Book* and *Black Book* of the Exchequer. The obligations described in the Inquest could not, he clearly saw (as Freeman and Stubbs had not), be an adaptation of the Anglo-Saxon 'military service of one fully-armed man for five hides' to the knight's fees of the Norman military tenants. He saw too (as Spelman long before had seen) the close connection of fully-developed military tenure with feudal incidents such as reliefs and wardships. But he was totally out of touch with the work of French scholars on Norman institutions, and approached the whole question of the purpose behind the 1087 and 1166 surveys from the point of view of a Victorian tax assessor. Moreover he failed, along with many other English historians, to appreciate the importance of non-feudal elements, in particular the permanent, trained and partly paid household troops, in the armies of the Norman kings.[43]

Round was never a writer of books. R. L. Poole, in search of an author for a projected 'Political History of England', said that he needed someone with 'the criticism of Round joined to the constructive gift he has not'.[44] But Round discovered in the *English Historical Review*, founded in 1886, an outlet both for his substantial articles and for his (often acrimonious) reviews criticising the work of others. Like the *American Historical Review*, founded in 1895, the *EHR* welcomed works based on rigorous research in original sources. Here too, in the book reviews (as Robin Fleming has shown of the *AHR*), 'a parade of wonderful, sharp, subversive critiques could be read that not only dealt with individual works but, more generally, with good history and bad'.[45] Poole, as editor, kept a firm hand on controversies; when Round had persisted too long in an attack on a minor point in Freeman's interpretation of the battle of Hastings, Poole announced that the discussion must be closed.[46] But for the most part, the review section provided a forum for debate on new interpretations of historical events, and helped to advance a more critical approach to history.

In spite of quarrels with many individual historians, Round was constructively involved in some new collective historical enterprises, notably the Victoria County Histories (launched in 1886) and the Pipe Roll Society (founded in 1883). His investigations into family history, added to his Domesday studies, made him an ideal contributor to the chapters on Domesday Book, published in translation for each county in the *VCH*; the introductions he wrote for twelve counties were some of the best in the series. His friendship with Maitland, broken only when Maitland wrote a review of Round's *Commune of London* that was not wholly favourable,[47] did not lead to active involvement with the Selden Society; and law, to his loss, was not one of his major interests. Round never took kindly to criticism; he reacted unfavourably to the suggestion of Delisle (in 1906) that a change in the style of Henry II's charters made it possible to revise the date of nine charters in Round's *Calendar of Documents preserved in France*. At the same time, he admitted that he was not an expert in diplomatic, writing, 'my own knowledge is empiric only; I had never any training whatever in the subject'.[48]

Round's *Calendar* was undertaken in response to the need for an Anglo-Norman cartulary, backed by Maxwell Lyte, the Deputy Keeper of the Public Record Office.[49] English historians had been slow to provide editions of documents relating to Normandy, including the charters of the Norman dukes, later kings of England. Indeed when systematic publication first began it was in the form of calendars, not full documents; not until 1961 did an edition of the charters of the Norman dukes up to 1066 appear, and then it was the work, not of an English, but of a French, scholar, Marie Fauroux.[50] The *Regesta* of William I and William II appeared in a calendar published in 1913; scholars have had to wait until 1998 for a complete edition of the *Charters of the Conquest*.[51] All this compared badly with the French editions of charters of their kings; and even though the charters of Henry II of England were being collected, publication was only partial, and once again was initiated by a French scholar, Léopold Delisle.[52] Still for all its faults Round's *Calendar* was a useful beginning. It was based for the most part on transcripts made by E. Deville, Léchaudé d'Anisy, and members of the École des Chartes, supplemented by Round in brief visits to Norman provincial archives and to the Bibliothèque Nationale. Inevitably there were many errors and omissions, due partly to the carelessness of Léchaudé d'Anisy, and partly to Round's haste and failure to take advantage of the work of contemporary French scholars.[53]

Before long much closer collaboration with both French and American historians helped to give a more balanced view of the nature and importance of the Norman Conquest. The collaboration had begun in the last decade of the nineteenth century, stimulated by the reviews and articles in the *EHR* and in the older academic magazines such as *The Athenaeum* as well as by the exchange of books and letters. Maitland's professional friendships took in European scholars including Liebermann and Vinogradoff, whose migration to Oxford when political conditions in Russia became difficult he encouraged.[54] American scholars too appear among his correspondents from an early date; he was writing in October 1885 to M. M. Bigelow, a legal historian who put together from chronicle and charter sources a collection of Anglo-Norman pleas from the time before records were systematically kept.[55] Bigelow's *Placita Anglo-Normannica*, published in 1879, was not superseded until the appearance of R. C. van Caenegem's two Selden Society volumes in 1990–91.[56]

Maitland's interests, wide as they were, were inclined towards law; and even in the *History of English Law*, which he began in collaboration with Pollock, he was prevented from giving full attention to the eleventh century through allowing Pollock to write the Anglo-Saxon chapters. He was unhappy with Pollock's work, and wrote as quickly as possible to prevent Pollock from writing anything more; but he was never able to give his full attention to the period of the Norman Conquest.[57] His wish to explore it more deeply was less than half satisfied by his work on Domesday Book. In the lectures he gave on 'Domesday Book and Beyond' he began to move back from 1087 to try to discover more about the law and society of Anglo-Saxon England; and with a surer sense of historical change than Round ever possessed he avoided imposing the later pattern of land ownership on the earlier period.[58] Maitland and Vinogradoff together, in their investigations into peasant society, helped to widen historical teaching, which was inclining too much towards constitutional and political history. Both, especially Vinogradoff, drew attention to the economic foundations of Anglo-Saxon society before the conquest, and opened up further investigation into changes in the lower ranks of the free and semi-free peasantry. The origins of the manor, the nature of serfdom and the disappearance of slavery, with all that this involved in social, legal, and even religious history, were now firmly on the agenda. The questions to ask of eleventh-century society were being rephrased. Finding the right questions was characteristic of the best historical work at the turn of the century; trying (not always successfully) to answer them was to be the work of the next generations.

Notes

1 Karl Marx, *The Communist Manifesto* (London, 1848), trans. S. Moore (Harmondsworth, Middlesex, 1967); P. Anderson, *Considerations on Western Marxism* (London, 1976); H. Fleischer, *Marxism and History* (London, 1973).
2 Walter Scott, *Ivanhoe*, cited in Asa Briggs, *Saxons, Normans and Victorians* (St Leonards-on-Sea, Sussex, 1966), pp. 10–11.
3 J. C. Holt, *Robin Hood* (Leicester, 1982), p. 183.

4 A. Thierry, *Histoire de la conquête de l'Angleterre par les Normands*, 2 vols (2nd edn, Paris, 1824), 1, p. viii.

5 S. Bertrand, 'The history of the Tapestry', in *The Bayeux Tapestry*, ed. Sir Frank Stenton (London, 1957), pp. 76–85, at pp. 79–81.

6 B. Disraeli, *Sybil, or, The Two Nations* (London, 1845; repr. Ware, Herts., 1995), p. 147.

7 P. Levine, *The Amateur and the Professional in Victorian England, 1838–1886* (Cambridge, 1986), p. 84.

8 George Borrow, *Wild Wales* (London, 1862; repr. Glasgow, 1977), p. 27; Charles Kingsley, 'The limits of exact science as applied to history', *The Roman and the Teuton: A Series of Lectures delivered before the University of Cambridge* (Cambridge and London, 1864).

9 O. Anderson, 'The political uses of history in mid-nineteenth-century England', *Past and Present* 36 (1967), pp. 87–105.

10 R. Jann, 'From amateur to professional: the case of the Oxbridge historians', *Journal of British Studies* 22 (1983), pp. 122–47.

11 M. D. Knowles, 'Great historical enterprises. 4: The Rolls Series', *TRHS*, 5th ser., 11 (1961), pp. 137–59.

12 *Ibid.*, pp. 158–9.

13 M. M. Condon and E. M. Hallam, 'Government printing of the Public Records in the nineteenth century', *Journal of the Society of Archivists* 7 (1984), pp. 348–88, at pp. 382–3; Levine, *Amateur and Professional*, p. 138.

14 David Bates, 'Léopold Delisle (1826–1910)', in *Medieval Scholarship. Biographical Studies on the Formation of a Discipline: 1. History*, eds H. Damico and J. B. Zavadil (New York and London, 1995), pp. 101–13, at pp. 101–2.

15 Robin Fleming, 'Picturesque history and the Medieval in nineteenth-century America', *The American Historical Review* 100 (1995), pp. 1061–94.

16 Jann, 'From amateur to professional', p. 138.

17 H. Butterfield, *Man on his Past* (Cambridge, 1955), pp. 72–4; see also Lord Acton, 'The German schools of history', *English Historical Review* 1 (1886), pp. 7–42, at pp. 28–9.

18 Levine, *Amateur and Professional*, p. 25; J. M. Kemble, *The Saxons in England: A History of the English Commonwealth till the period of the Norman Conquest* (London, 1849).

19 Levine, *Amateur and Professional*, pp. 79, 116.

20 Benjamin Thorpe, *History of England under the Saxon Kings* (London, 1845).

21 J. F. A. Mason, 'William Stubbs', in *The Blackwell Dictionary of Historians*, ed. John Cannon, R. H. C. Davis, W. Doyle, J. P. Greene (Oxford, 1988), pp. 395–6; W. H. Hudson, *Letters of William Stubbs, Bishop of Oxford, 1825–1901* (London, 1904).

22 *Select Charters and other illustrations of English Constitutional History from the Earliest Times to the Reign of Edward the First*, ed. W. Stubbs (Oxford, 1870), Preface.

23 W. Stubbs, *The Constitutional History of England*, 3 vols, 3rd edn (Oxford, 1873–78), 1, p. 2.

24 *Ibid.*, 1, p. 10.

25 *Ibid.*, 1. pp. 250–2.
26 J. F. A. Mason, 'Edward Augustus Freeman', in *The Blackwell Dictionary of Historians*, pp. 139–40; H. A. Cronne, 'Edward Augustus Freeman', in *History*, n.s. 28 (1943), pp. 48–92.
27 Cited in Levine, *Amateur and Professional*, p. 81.
28 Mason, 'Freeman', p. 140.
29 E. A. Freeman, *The Norman Conquest of England*, 6 vols (Oxford, 1867–79), 1, p. 593.
30 *Ibid.*, 2, p. 515.
31 *The Letters of Frederic William Maitland*, ed. C. H. S. Fifoot, Selden Society (London, 1965), no. 209 (p. 210).
32 F. M. Stenton, *Anglo-Saxon England* (Oxford, 1943; 2nd edn, 1947), pp. 702–3, 'As an introduction to the sources for the political history of the period, the book is of great and permanent value'.
33 D. C. Douglas, *The Norman Conquest and the British Historians* (Glasgow, 1946); Ann Williams, *The English and the Norman Conquest* (Woodbridge, Suffolk, 1995).
34 W. Page, 'Memoir of Dr J. Horace Round', in *Family Origins and other Studies*, ed. W. Page (London, 1930); E. J. King, 'John Horace Round and the *Calendar of Documents preserved in France*', *Anglo-Norman Studies* 4 (1981), pp. 93–103, 202–4.
35 See below, p. 63.
36 *The Anarchy of King Stephen's Reign*, ed. Edmund King (Oxford, 1994), pp. vii–viii.
37 J. H. Round, *Geoffrey de Mandeville* (London, 1892), p. v .
38 Stubbs, *Constitutional History*, 1, pp. 327–8.
39 Round, *Geoffrey de Mandeville*, p. vi.
40 Freeman, *Norman Conquest*, 1, p. viii.
41 J. H. Round, *Feudal England* (London, 1909), p. 317.
42 *Ibid.*, p. 225.
43 See below, pp. 85–6.
44 Fifoot, *Letters of Maitland*, p. 291, n.1.
45 Fleming, 'Picturesque history', p. 1085.
46 *English Historical Review* 9 (1894), p. 611.
47 F. W. Maitland, review of *The Commune of London*, in *The Athenaeum*, 21 Oct. 1899, to which Round wrote 'a peevish rejoinder' in *The Athenaeum*, 28 Oct. 1899. See Fifoot, *Letters of Maitland*, no. 252 (p. 252).
48 King, 'Round and The *Calendar*', p. 103.
49 *Ibid.*, pp. 94–5.
50 *Recueil des actes des ducs de Normandie (911–1066)*, ed. M. Fauroux, Mémoires de la Société des Antiquaires de Normandie, 96 (Caen, 1961).
51 *Regesta Regum Anglo-Normannorum, 1066–1087*, ed. David Bates (Oxford, 1998).
52 *Recueil des actes de Henri II concernant les provinces françaises et les affaires de France*, ed. L. Delisle and E. Berger, 3 vols (Paris, 1909–27).
53 King, 'Round and the *Calendar*', pp. 97–101.
54 Fifoot, *Letters of Maitland*; and P. N. R. Zutshi, *The Letters of Frederic William Maitland*, vol. 2, Selden Soc. (London, 1995).

55 M. M. Bigelow, *Placita Anglo-Normannica* (London, 1879).
56 R. C. van Caenegem, *English Lawsuits from William I to Richard I*, 2 vols, Selden Society, 106, 107 (London, 1990–91).
57 F. Pollock and F. W. Maitland, *The History of English Law before the Time of Edward I* (Cambridge, 1895; 2nd edn, with an introduction by S. F. C. Milson, 1968); Fifoot, *Letters of Maitland*, no. 109, to Paul Vinogradoff.
58 F. W. Maitland, *Domesday Book and Beyond* (Cambridge, 1897).

5

The early twentieth century

Throughout the twentieth century historical writing in Britain, France and North America was professional and university based. This was not true of totalitarian states, where history was harnessed to propaganda. Elsewhere, even though the view of Benedetto Croce that 'all history is contemporary history' might be accepted, it was usually in the sense that the preoccupations of the present would influence the questions asked of the past. Leading historical journals such as the *English Historical Review* and the *American Historical Review* took a strong line in rejecting works 'fashioned to engage in modern political debates'; and S. R. Gardiner asserted, 'He who studies the history of the past will be of greater service to the society of the present in proportion as he leaves it out of account'.[1] Current interests were important influences on the way that history was written; changing philosophical ideas and new scientific approaches encouraged historians to rethink their interpretations of past events. The 'chain of cause and effect' – which even Maitland had tacitly accepted – gave way to a more 'ecological' or 'holistic' view of history. Social history and 'history from below', already pioneered pragmatically by J. R. Green,[2] were reshaped by techniques taken over from other disciplines, such as sociology and anthropology. In the last three decades of the century the new techniques of analysis made possible by computer technology helped to clarify medieval sources. For the Norman Conquest and its consequences these were particularly important in penetrating the obscurities of Domesday Book and other related surveys. There were debates and disagreements between historians, but even when they became passionate they were rarely motivated by politics.

In the first decade of the century studies of the Norman Conquest became increasingly international. At first American influence was felt most strongly through the study of Norman institutions, hitherto either neglected by English historians, or investigated for their relevance to the loss of Normandy in 1204, not to 1066.[3] The pioneer in the field was Charles Homer Haskins. In 1902 he began a systematic tour of the French archives in search of early documentary sources. Unlike his pragmatic English contemporaries, he went with the kind of training in diplomatic and palaeography to which the French were accustomed in their École des Chartes, and which was becoming available in American universities. Whereas J. H. Round had never been at home in his perfunctory and somewhat peevish canters through the French archives, Haskins spent long and reflective days examining the records and forming friendships with archivists and historians, notably Léopold Delisle, administrator general of the Bibliothèque Nationale.[4] When in 1917 he wrote the preface to his *Norman Institutions*, published the following year, he gratefully recorded the memories that the work recalled: memories 'not so much of dusty *fonds d'archives* or weary journeys on the Ouest–État, as of quiet days of study in provincial collections, long evenings of reflection by the Orne or the Vire or in the garden of some cathedral city, and rare afternoons at Chantilly with Léopold Delisle'.[5] The Normans as a force in European history fired his imagination, and even before he completed his book on Normandy he had published (in 1915) a more general work on *The Normans in European History*.[6]

In approaching the history of the duchy of Normandy itself, Haskins wrote:

> The institutions of the duchy of Normandy occupy a unique place in the history of Europe. They have their local interest, giving character and distinctness to an important region of France; they furnished models of orderly and centralized administration to the French kings after the conquest of the duchy by Philip Augustus; and they exerted an influence of the first importance upon the constitutional and legal development of England and the countries of English law. Normandy was thus the channel through which the stream of

Frankish and feudal custom flowed to England; it was the training ground where the first Anglo-Norman king gained his experience as a ruler, and the source whence his followers drew their ideas of law and government; and during nearly a century and a half of personal union with England it afforded a constant example of parallel development.[7]

He explained that he had undertaken his studies with a view to seeking light on the constitutional development of England (though he had discovered much that bore only indirectly on that), and added that there was a lack of sufficient information for a full constitutional history of Normandy: the surviving records were too fragmentary. He hoped, nevertheless, to have given a comprehensive description of the government of Normandy on the eve of the conquest, and to have reached new conclusions on the military, fiscal and judicial organisation of the duchy.

Haskins's work brought Normandy into the centre of conquest studies. In his exploration of Norman archives he began by following Round. His first two weeks of work, however, shook his confidence in Round's *Calendar*. 'It isn't anything like complete', he wrote to a colleague, 'even for Normandy; and for Anjou and Touraine the lacunae are considerable'.[8] Fortunately, by attributing its failings to the lack of facilities given to Round, he avoided getting into controversy with a touchy opppontent, and Round welcomed the publication of *Norman Institutions*. One point of agreement was the question of the imposition of knight service, not wholly surprising, since Haskins followed Round in starting from the later (1172) returns of service due from Norman tenants-in-chief and working back to the mid-eleventh century. After studying the obligations of ecclesiastical tenants, he observed that military service was due from only nine monasteries, all but one of which were founded before the Conqueror's accession.[9] After further analysis, he concluded that the military obligations must have been imposed as early as the time of Duke Robert, and thence he went on by stages to confirm Round's view that 'the Normans were familiar with *servitium debitum* in terms of the ten-knight unit when they landed in England'.[10] He looked too for early evidence for the existence of feudal aids and a forty days' period of obligatory service. This was pioneering work; many of the charters and records that Haskins perused were still unpublished, though some records escaped his notice; and he might have come to different conclusions if he could have had at hand the volume of early ducal charters published much later by Marie Fauroux. As it was, his authority bolstered Round's theory of the introduction of knight-service into England, and had a lasting and by no means beneficial influence on academic study for several decades.

By putting new emphasis on the Normans, Haskins helped to enlarge the topics for investigation. It seemed to him likely that the character and experience of the Norman conquerors in England would have influenced the other regions that they conquered, notably southern Italy.[11] He regretted the lack of evidence that would have allowed him to compare the conditions in the parts of Italy conquered by the Normans; though the *Catalogus baronum* of the mid-twelfth century appeared to be based on groups of five and ten knights,[12] and other evidence pointed to the existence of feudal aids and of a forty days' period of service. 'These parallelisms', he suggested, 'are so close that they can be satisfactorily explained only by treating the feudalism of the South as an offshoot from the parent stem in Normandy in the early period of Norman expansion'. In this way he helped to direct studies along lines suggested in the 1890s, while at the same time widening the areas of investigation to include the place of Normandy and England in Europe. Both subjects invited controversy.

While Haskins was bringing Norman institutions into the debate, his contemporary, F. M. Stenton, widened it with new work on Anglo-Saxon and Scandinavian influences. Stenton appreciated the contribution of Round; in his 1929 Ford Lectures he commented on 'the remarkable movement which, rather more than thirty years ago, created the modern study of English feudal institutions', citing the work of Maitland, Liebermann in his *Gesetze*, and Round.[13] There had, he noted, naming Stapleton and Eyton, been great genealogists before Round, but he had shown how essential genealogy was to feudal institutions.

Round's work, however, Stenton insisted, had been incomplete. 'He accepted the existence of a centralized feudal state in England without inquiring into its origin. He gave little ... attention to the internal organization of the individual honours of which that society was composed, and he was always inclined to regard the independent action of a twelfth-century baron as an encroachment upon royal authority'. Moreover, 'he was perhaps too ready to assume that King William and his sons had controlled feudal justice and feudal administration as they certainly controlled the military organization which they had created for the defence of the realm'.[14] To go more deeply into early English institutions, to study with still greater technical expertise the mass of still unpublished charters, and to widen knowledge of local settlements and local variations of custom through place-name studies, was to be Stenton's achievement.[15] Haskins's work was to be taken up and expanded by David Douglas, whose studies too were focused on the Normans and their achievements in Normandy, England and Southern Italy; it contributed in a new way to the 'Normans versus English' debate.[16]

Meanwhile, work published by T. F. Tout on the central administration was carried on by his pupil V. H. Galbraith, who brought unrivalled knowledge of the Public Record Office and the diplomatic of early charters to bear on the interpretation of medieval English history. Galbraith's early interest in the fourteenth century was remote from conquest studies; but the last thirty years of his life were devoted more and more to the study of Domesday Book.[17] His paper on this subject, published in the *English Historical Review* in 1942 began a new interpretation of the way the survey had been carried out, and led in time to two major books on the making of Domesday Book and an edition of the 'Herefordshire Domesday'.[18]

Galbraith's work always began from documents; indeed he wrote that 'the only way to understand the past is to study the sources at first hand'. The documents that were important to him were not merely the administrative records which he had known in the Public Record Office; chronicles were equally important. Some of his earliest work was on the St Albans Chronicle; and when he was elected to a chair in Edinburgh he enlisted the willing help of Peter Morison, managing director of Thomas Nelson and Sons to found the series of Nelson's Medieval Texts (later transferred to Oxford as the Oxford Medieval Texts).

Critical editions of Latin chronicles with *en face* English translations were undertaken by scholars: these books, as he wrote, 'are the very stuff of history, which no substitute can replace'. He himself, in Edinburgh, London, and finally Oxford, was one of the most influential and certainly the liveliest of teachers of medieval history: a practical exponent of his belief that 'history, surely, is the living knowledge in living minds, a common awareness of the past by teachers and taught, a search for truth ever changing as error is corrected and more is discovered'.[19]

The most significant studies of English and Norman history in the middle years of the twentieth century were based on the work of Round, Maitland, Haskins and Stenton, extended in that of Galbraith and Douglas. David Douglas had been a research pupil of Vinogradoff, and his early interests were in social studies; a special interest in the Normans first emerged when he wrote 'his most original book', *English Scholars,* which included a study of the historiography of the Norman Conquest. It was, however, his friendship with the learned and reticent scholar, Lewis Loyd, that first directed his attention to Anglo-Norman history. Loyd, as Douglas later wrote, 'with characteristic generosity allowed me to profit without stint from his instruction, and from his own researches'. From that time the Normans, in Normandy no less than in England, and in the Mediterranean world, dominated his historical work. His books were influential in placing the conquest in its wider, European, setting.[20]

The questions asked were at first focused on the institutions of both England and Normandy, with a view to deciding how far they influenced each other. Royal power was still one central theme, as it had been for centuries; alongside was the question of restraints on that power, of the authority of the royal council, whether witenagemot or feudal *curia*, and of the restraining force of law or custom. Feudal rights and obligations were balanced against long-standing public rights. Seignorial power was a related issue. The arguments were widened as historians made increasing use of the disciplines of the social sciences. But, even when arguments became passionate, they remained academic, concerned essentially to discover the truth. While many special studies were based on analysis and careful weighing of sources, they were often distorted and oversimplified in discussion. The nature of university teaching, which necessarily involved working towards examinations, sometimes sharpened controversies. In 1963 Keith Thomas referred to the disfigurement caused by 'the rhetoric and impressionism which is so frequently encountered in the work of leading practitioners of modern history (and whose origin may well lie in the educational tradition of encouraging history undergraduates to produce dogmatic and personal interpretations on the basis of rapid reading in the secondary sources)'.[21] Distortion through generalisation was, fortunately, balanced by the much subtler and less confrontational work of serious historians. And behind the controversies many historians were quietly deepening their knowledge of underlying social structures.

Comparative studies multiplied in the second and third quarters of the twentieth century. Archaeology was to many historians an essential allied discipline: R. Allen Brown used to insist to his students that 'archaeologists are really historians', and their work was found invaluable for the history of castles and churches, the study of field systems and urban development, and much more. Without at first adopting the techniques of other disciplines, historians began more and more frequently to ask the kind of questions asked by sociologists and anthropologists. Comparative studies became frequent. There had been earlier hints of these preoccupations; indeed the writers of the Scottish enlightenment, including Robertson, Hume and Adam Smith, had speculated about comparative development. Seebohm and Green had introduced economic history into their work; Maitland had broken away from rigid chronological development, working critically from the known to the unknown in *Domesday Book and Beyond*. Vinogradoff had brought a more sociological approach when he left Moscow for Oxford in 1903. And it must never be forgotten that, as J. C. Holt pointed out later, 'family relations played a part in historical explanation long before their apotheosis in the pages of the *Annales* and the work of the Freiburg school'.[22] They were, indeed a substantial part of the work of historians from Robert of Torigni to countless local historians in England and Normandy; and in 1892 Round published, in his *Geoffrey de Mandeville* 'the first systematic application of genealogical study to political history'.[23]

The conscious use of new techniques for studying comparative development, when it emerged, was at first most marked on
the European continent. In 1929 Marc Bloch and Lucien Febvre
founded the journal *Annales d'histoire économique et sociale*
(later renamed *Annales: économies, société, civilisation*), which
has been seen as the origin of the *Annales* school of history. Its
avowed aim was to break away from 'the idol of narrative,
chronological history', which had dominated historical writing in
the previous century.[24] At first it found more supporters on the
continent of Europe than in England or North America, though a
few historians, notably M. M. Postan and Eileen Power, were
making it known through their seminars in London. The full
impact reached England with the founding of *Past and Present* in
1952.

Sociology at first met with some active opposition from historians, notably E. P. Thompson, whose book on *The Making of the
English Working Class* (1963) was of fundamental importance in
the development of social history. His attack on sociology,
however, was directed against the earlier writings of its practitioners, which, as Philip Abrams pointed out, had been 'flawed by
a radically unsound methodology'.[25] This was due to the way
they used types of structural systems, including industrialism,
feudalism and legal–national authority. Even though some of
their polarities – status and contract, community and association,
the folk-community and the urban community – helped in identifying changes, they easily led to 'research on myths which
sociologists have invented'.[26] He cited the example of one
research unit which spent some years in 'proving the non-exis-
tence in pre-industrial England and elsewhere of a type of family
unit which no-one familiar with the historical evidence ever said
did exist'.

Even before Abrams wrote to explain the earlier misconcep-
tions, historians had begun to appreciate the constructive ways in
which they might use the newer disciplines. In an article on
'History and anthropology', published in 1963. Keith Thomas
had observed that the two disciplines were drawing closer
together; he pointed to the greater precision of anthropology,
and to the way in which the anthropologist, however specialised
his study of a subject, always made it against a background of his

conception of the social system to which it was related.[27] More generally, even the most pragmatic historians – though not adopting the techniques of sociologists and anthropologists – tended to investigate the same subjects more consciously. They wrote readily on such topics as oral culture and myth, domination and order. Within thirty years it was possible for Richard J. Evans to write, 'Virtually everything of meaning or importance to contemporary humanity now has a written history'.[28] These new approaches helped to encourage a great outburst of writing on the Norman Conquest, further stimulated by the ninth centenaries of the Battle of Hastings in 1966 and Domesday Book twenty years later. Older controversies still persisted, but they were progressively modified.

Notes

1 Cited in Robin Fleming, 'Picturesque history and the Medieval in nineteenth-century America', *The American Historical Review* 100 (1995), pp. 1061–94, at p. 1094.

2 J. R. Green, *A Short History of England* (London, 1874). Green's method met at first with hostility from fellow historians. Freeman wrote in a letter to Green, 'To my notions you have largely sacrificed the real stuff to your power of brilliant *talkee-talkee*' (unpublished letter, cited in P. Levine, *The Amateur and the Professional* (Cambridge, 1986), p. 27.

3 F. M. Powicke, *The Loss of Normandy, 1189–1204* (Manchester, 1913; 2nd edn, 1963); *Magni Rotuli Scaccarii Normanniae sub Regibus Angliae*, ed. Thomas Stapleton, Society of Antiquaries (London, 1940–44).

4 E. J. King, 'John Horace Round and the *Calendar of Documents preserved in France*', *Anglo-Norman Studies* 4 (1981), pp. 93–103.

5 C. H. Haskins, *Norman Institutions* (Cambridge, Massachusetts, 1925), p. x.

6 C. H. Haskins, *The Normans in European History* (London, 1916).

7 Haskins, *Norman Institutions*, p. viii.

8 King, 'Round and the *Calendar*', p. 101.

9 Haskins, *Norman Institutions*, p. 9.

10 *Ibid.*, p. 18.

11 *Ibid.*, pp. 23–4.

12 Details of service owed to the Norman kings of Sicily were recorded in the *Catalogus baronum* of the mid-twelfth century. This was later published by Evelyn Jamison: *Catalogus baronum*, ed. Evelyn Jamison, Fonti per la Storia d'Italia, 101 (Rome, 1972); it shows the development of military service in Norman Italy a century after the coming of the Normans. Some details are provided in Miss Jamison's supplement to the *Catalogus*, published after her death: 'Additional work on the *Catalogus Baronum*', in Evelyn M. Jamison, *Studies in the History of Medieval Sicily and South Italy*, eds Dione Clementi and Theo Kölzer (Aalen, 1992), pp. 523–85, especially pp. 526–8.

13 F. M. Stenton, *The First Century of English Feudalism, 1066–1166* (Oxford, 1932; 2nd edn, 1961), pp. 1–2.

14 *Ibid.*, p. 3.

15 The range and detail of Stenton's studies are indicated in the bibliography of his works in *Preparatory to Anglo-Saxon England*, ed. D. M. Stenton (Oxford, 1970), pp. viii–xiv. Among the most important of his documentary studies are *Documents illustrative of the Social and Economic History of the Danelaw*, British Academy, Records of the Social and Economic History of England and Wales (London, 1920) and *Transcripts of Charters relating to Gilbertine Houses*, Lincoln Record Society, 18 (Lincoln, 1922), the Introduction to which provided the best brief introduction to the diplomatic of English charters for several generations of students.

16 D. C. Douglas, *William the Conqueror* (London, 1964); D. C. Douglas, *The Norman Achievement, 1050–1100* (London, 1969; reissued, 1972).

17 As early as 1936 Galbraith told me he was coming to the conclusion that once you got into Domesday Book you never got out of it.

18 V. H. Galbraith, *The Making of Domesday Book* (Oxford, 1961); V. H. Galbraith, *Domesday Book: Its Place in Administrative History* (Oxford, 1974); *The Herefordshire Domesday*, eds V. H. Galbraith and James Tait, Pipe Roll Society (London, 1950); V. H. Galbraith, 'The Making of Domesday Book', *English Historical Review* 57 (1941), pp. 161–77.

19 Quotations from V. H. Galbraith, 'Afterthought', in *The Historian's Workshop*, ed. L. P. Curtis, Jr (New York, 1970), pp. 4–21.

20 The details of his life and publications are given in the 'Memoir' by R. H. C. Davis, *Proceedings of the British Academy* 69 (1983), pp. 513–42.

21 Keith Thomas, 'History and anthropology', *Past and Present* 24 (1963), pp. 3–24, at p. 5.

22 J. C. Holt, 'Patronage and politics', *TRHS*, 5th ser., 34 (1984), pp. 1–25, at p. 2.

23 *Ibid.*, p. 3.

24 Traian Stoianovich, 'The Annales School', *The Blackwell Dictionary of Historians*, ed. John Cannon, R. H. C. Davis, W. Doyle, J. P. Greene (Oxford, 1988), pp. 10–12 (with bibliography).

25 Philip Abrams, 'The sense of the past and the origins of sociology', *Past and Present* 55 (1972), p. 18.

26 *Ibid.*, p. 29.

27 K. Thomas, 'History and anthropology', p. 6.

28 Richard J. Evans, *In Defence of History* (London, 1997), p. 165.

6

The later twentieth century: from feudalism to lordship

Feudalism is a good word, and will cover a multitude of ignorances.

F. W. Maitland

During the last four decades of the twentieth century the approach of historians to the Norman Conquest continued to change. Of primary importance was the move away from the dominance of 'feudalism' in the military aspect, which Round had forced on historical studies. Up to that time most historians had fallen into the habit of writing unquestionably about feudalism and the feudal system. Both Pocock and Douglas in discussing Spelman's definitions of 'feudal custom' and 'feudal law' (Spelman never used the word 'feudalism'), hailed him as almost modern in his approach. Pocock wrote in 1957 of eighteenth-century historiography:

> It could be said ... that the heirs of Spelman died beaten and broken men, perishing among the spears of triumphant Whiggery. With their defeat ended the first serious attempt to give feudalism its proper place in English history, and there was not another until the nineteenth century, when the task was successfully accomplished by historians whom we may feel to be still our contemporaries.[1]

In fact the undermining of the whole feudal interpretation of the Norman Conquest became apparent soon after Pocock wrote.

In the first place, historians were looking critically at the actual course of the conquest itself, and at the condition of Normandy before 1066. R. H. C. Davis, in a short and perceptive summing-up of the Norman Conquest in 1966, pointed out on the military side that 'for some time the Normans lived as an "army of occupation" based on their castles with their household knights. The date at which it would have been safe for the household knights to be enfeoffed and live on their own lands would have varied'.[2] D. C. Douglas, in 1964, challenged the view of Haskins that 'Norman society in 1066 is a feudal society, and one of the most fully developed feudal societies in Europe'. On the contrary, he argued that 'such definition as was attained in the duchy during the Conqueror's reign is recorded for the most part in Norman charters after the conquest of England'.[3] Jean Yver was even more explicit in his address to the Spoleto conference in 1968 when, citing Douglas, he suggested that perhaps the Norman feudal and military system was developed only after the conquest of England, in imitation of the more logical order that William had been able to impose in a conquered country.[4] The terms 'feudalism' and 'feudal system' continued to be used, even by those historians who questioned their wholesale importation from one country to another; but the meaning of the terms themselves was coming more and more under direct attack.

J. C. Holt expressed the feelings of many historians when he wrote in 1986, 'We seem no longer to believe in feudalism, let alone the notion that it was established at a single stroke'.[5] Historians writing of different countries and periods usually found it necessary to explain just what they meant when using the term. Chris Wickham, writing of Europe generally, argued that the 'feudal mode ... did not require the extinction of all political power; Normandy and Norman England, as "feudo-vassalic" as any society, show an undiminished political power that certainly had Carolingian (and Anglo-Saxon) roots, though the mode of expression had changed'.[6] His definition treated political units as feudal if they were 'based on the politics and economics of landowning'. This was a far looser definition of 'feudal' than Spelman – or those who wrote in the legal tradition derived from Spelman – would have allowed.

One unexpected consequence of the cross-fertilisation of disciplines in the twentieth century was that technical terms such as 'concept', 'model', or 'construct', proper to philosophy, economics, sociology, or even literary criticism, slipped into the vocabulary of historians, to be used by them in ways that were neither rigorous nor consistent. When applied to such generalisations as 'feudalism' or 'imperialism' they helped to generate misunderstanding. In his 1941 Cambridge lectures, Postan described the manor as 'a concept'. A few years later the word 'model' had crept into seminar discussions of both manorialism and feudalism. When in 1974 E. A. R. Brown denounced the dominance of feudalism in historical writing, she described it as 'the tyranny of a construct',[7] so replacing philosophical and economic terms by one more familiar in literary criticism. It invited the immediate 'deconstruction' of feudalism. This came from several directions, notably from Susan Reynolds, who launched a comprehensive frontal attack in 1994 on the blinkered discussion resulting from the feudal approach to medieval studies.

In *Fiefs and Vassals* (1994), Reynolds set out to determine 'how far vassalage and the fief as they are generally understood, constituted institutions which are definable, comprehensible, and helpful to the understanding of medieval history,' and argued that 'in so far as they are definable and comprehensible, they are not helpful'.[8] Her book looked at the subject across medieval western Europe (excluding Catalonia) and, whereas some of its general assertions have been questioned, the section on eleventh- and twelfth-century England has made a useful contribution to the debate on the effects of the Norman Conquest. Starting from the views of seventeenth-century pamphleteers and lawyers that (in different ways) 'the Normans had subverted Anglo-Saxon liberties', she pointed out that, especially since Round's essay on the introduction of knight service, the debate had 'been conducted on rather a narrow front'. Many historians had focused on military service and 'a hierarchy of tenure or property rights'.[9] Looking at the evidence of Domesday Book, she noted that, although the king undoubtedly gave out properties wholesale, 'not all properties were given out as tidily as the myth requires'; also that 'fief' or 'fee' was not synonymous with 'knight's fee'.[10] Many holdings 'in feodo' or 'ad feodum' in Domesday Book were small, and some paid rent. There was no evidence that a precise definition of service formed an automatic part of each grant. Much of this was not new, but it needed to be said. Her arguments provided a comprehensive rebuttal of the assertion (still occasionally made) that William established 'a perfect feudal pyramid' in England.

Such a statement shows the malign influence of feudal 'models' at their very worst, and the rebuttal is salutary.

A book of such wide content and combative assertions was bound to provide discussion and controversy. Frederick L. Cheyette, in a searching review in *Speculum*,[11] questioned some of Reynolds's assumptions, and found some of her interpretations strange and even misguided; but at the same time he welcomed the book for the thoroughgoing critique of the conventional concept of feudalism, that would force historians to reconsider their views on fundamental questions about the Middle Ages. Further discussion of some of the main issues appeared almost at once in a debate on 'The feudal revolution' in *Past and Present*.[12] Much of this debate was, naturally, concerned with the continental background which had made up a large part of Reynolds's book. It brought out the newer methods of looking at the social and institutional changes of the Middle Ages, which had already gone a long way to undermine the older conception of feudalism. T. N. Bisson was particularly concerned with power and lordship, suggesting a new acceptance of noble lordship as the basis of social order.[13] Timothy Reuter, though finding the stress on lordship helpful, criticised the way European history had been written from the point of view of France and the breakdown of public order there. Looking at the effect of the Norman Conquest in England, he pointed out (though questioning the 'maximalist' view of the Old English state) that the royal grip on the polity was tight enough to be taken over simply by capturing its central apparatus.[14] Chris Wickham raised the fundamental question of how far a given society, in contrast with another, is more usefully described in terms of one ideal type (for example, Carolingian) rather than another (such as feudal). In considering the debate about 1066, he suggested that there were two changes which were important at the time. The first was the changing relationship between local aristocratic power and wider political forces, such as those controlled by kings, dukes or bishops (which had been discussed by Bisson). The second was the development of increasingly explicit and formal personal relationships.[15]

Indeed, much of the work of serious historians in the two decades before the appearance of Reynolds's book had already been concerned with questions of this kind, rather than with the older controversies concealed under the arid word, feudalism. As Maitland had said long before of feudalism, it 'covers a multitude of ignorances'. As for the changes produced by the Norman Conquest, Reynolds herself granted that recent work (for instance that of J. C. Holt and John Gillingham) had shown that the existence of immediate and systematic change looks weaker than Round had maintained.[16] Perhaps the persistence of theories long after they had been undermined in serious scholarship was due to the over-simplification of work directed to answering examination questions, of which Keith Thomas had complained.[17] Much of the historical writing generated in part by the 1066 and 1086 centenaries was concerned with a much deeper and more critical examination of the gradual changes over the divide of the conquest. This included much research which focused on 'individuals in their particular, complex network of relationships and ... the systematic practices and transactions in which they are engaged'.[18]

The rejection of 'feudalism' has not involved the rejection of the adjective 'feudal'. Lordship and tenure were of immense importance; they influenced almost every aspect of law and society after the conquest. Writing of the Salisbury oaths and the Domesday Survey, J. C. Holt drew attention to Martin Wright's *Introduction to the Law of Tenures* (1730), where he suggested that 'Domesday and the Salisbury oath marked the introduction of feudal tenures'; an idea developed by Blackstone in his *Commentaries*.[19] On 1 August 1086, William the Conqueror, as one version of the *Anglo-Saxon Chronicle* relates,

> came to Salisbury, and his council came to him, and all the landholding men of any account throughout England, whosoever men they were, and they all bowed down to him and became his men, and swore oaths of fealty to him that they would be faithful to him against all other men.[20]

To the question 'for what did they perform homage'? Holt, arguing that by this date the survey on which Domesday Book was based had already been completed, and that homage was then 'part of a reciprocal act ... not performed *in vacuo* or for the promise of good lordship, but in return for something material and real',[21] proposed that the oaths secured the tenures of both tenants-in-chief and undertenants in the lands granted to them at various times and in various ways in England.[22] The book was used to determine tenure throughout the next two centuries.[23]

This is not to imply that William introduced that historical chimera, a 'perfect feudal pyramid'. The oaths 'against all other men' on which William insisted were directed, Holt proposes, particularly against the king of France. The suggestion that the Domesday survey might have been made before the oaths were taken is also considered by Elizabeth Hallam and H. B. Clarke, and there is still an active debate on the subject.[24] The discussion has gained by the reintroduction of the 'Salisbury oaths' as a topic for consideration. It could be added that there were lateral no less than vertical ties: undertenants sometimes had more than one lord to whom they had obligations. Judith Green has given illustrations of some multiple dependencies, as well as of obligations arising from affinity rather than tenure.[25] As late as the fourteenth century any tenant of Lilleshall Abbey, taking an oath to the abbot his lord for admission to his lands, would swear fealty to him 'saving only the fealty which I owe to my lord the king and to my other lords'.[26] As Lindy Grant pointed out in demolishing Lemarignier's suggestion that Abbot Suger of St-Denis invented a feudal hierarchy in France, the abbot's approach was political and pragmatic.[27] The Normans in England too were essentially pragmatic. Lordship was only one of the bonds of society, even when tied to land; there were also ducal rights and royal rights, which were part of the ruler's power. Lordship had, however, an important place in many social and legal relationships.

The military side of the conquest was not – and could not have been – neglected, for military power made the conquest possible, and continued to sustain the Anglo-Norman kingdom in its early years. It was, however, looked at in the wider context of social history, and with a clearer understanding of the condition of Normandy before 1066. The appearance of a critical edition of the charters of the Norman dukes in 1961 made possible a re-evaluation of the evidence that had misled Haskins half a century earlier. A wealth of new charter evidence showed that no uniform system of *servicium debitum* had been imposed by the Norman dukes; there was no system that could have been introduced into England. The military duties of vassalage were being worked out; the practical need to maintain a substantial army ready at all times to take the field hastened the imposition of more precise demands for service on the greatest lords who had been enriched with huge estates in England, and on the ecclesiastical tenants-in-chief as well. But the king recognised very soon after the conquest that demands made in terms of knights could when convenient be converted into money; and commutation, in the form of scutage, was calculated on the basis of the knight's fee. Indeed, as J. H. Prestwich had shown as early as 1954, military service was never confined within the limits of the *servicium debitum* and the older English *fyrd*.[28] Paid troops were at least equally important; the military households of the Norman kings contained the most highly-trained units in their armies. They were essential for manning castles and providing the core of resistance to attack in the rare battles and frequent sieges. In times of crisis the royal armies were augmented by the military households of the leading barons. These men relied on regular wages, as did the large contingents of mercenaries, often Breton or Flemish, recruited by the kings in special emergencies. Richard fitz Nigel, writing the *Dialogue of the Exchequer* in the reign of Henry II, asserted that 'the wealth that accrues to kings by virtue of their position gives power'.[29] The security of the realm, he pointed out, depended upon its wealth, for money was indispensable in both peace and war. 'In war it is lavished on fortifying castles, paying soldiers' wages, and innumerable other expenses'. He did not need to dwell on the economic conditions necessary to produce the wealth. As Prestwich clearly showed, the royal household, which contained the king's chief administrative officers as well as the commanders of his knights, was linked to the provision of men and money for war.[30]

One aspect of the military household was given prominence by Georges Duby, in his seminal 1964 article on 'Youth in aristocratic society'.[31] He brought out the importance of the household in aristocratic society, both as a training ground for knights and as a career for younger sons. Mounted warfare depended on long and continuous training of men and horses, best provided in a permanent military force. So household troops included the eldest sons of barons waiting to succeed to their inheritance, as well as the younger sons (both legitimate and illegitimate) who hoped by good service to be given estates of their own or the hand of an heiress. All came from families able to provide the essential equipment of horse and armour, even though some were from relatively poor families. So there was an element of social standing among knights, although essentially they were professional in their skills.[32]

Published work on the military aspects of the Norman Conquest has been concerned with many aspects of war and its place in society. Inevitably, the influence of the Norman Conquest has been one element in this work. But the heat has gone out of the debate; the historical paper battles of Round's day have given way to a calmer (if sometimes acerbic) attempt to assess the nature of the changes in the light of new material published, or older sources made more accessible in new editions and translations. On the military side, some fifteen recent articles were brought together with a useful introduction by Matthew Strickland in *Anglo-Norman Warfare*;[33] and many more on a wide variety of topics have appeared in the published proceedings of conferences. The Battle conferences in Anglo-Norman Studies were initiated and inspired by R. A. Brown in 1978,[34] and have since their inception provided a forum for debate, amicable disagreement, and often consensus for scholars from different disciplines. They have been followed by an American series of conferences held by the Haskins Society.[35] The French have not been backward; a series of *colloques* organised by the University of Caen have taken place at Cerisy.[36] Military tactics, the logistics of the conquest, and the character of fortifications before and after 1066 have been discussed in much greater detail.[37] Much of the work of historians is now focused on the effect of the conquest on such topics as lordship, law and the family. Sometimes the approach is suggested by issues of contemporary importance in a different society, such as race and peoples, colonisation and frontiers, as well as the wider question of Anglo-Norman England in Europe.

In all the various studies, lordship remains a central issue. It is bound up with power and law enforcement as well as with household organisation and administrative development. Lordship also involves the question of the fate of the English at all levels of society after the conquest. There has been broad general agreement on the disastrous losses of the English aristocracy after their defeat at Hastings; the questions are how far the changes were effected by due process of law, and what happened in the lower ranks of society. Within twenty years the change at the highest level had been so sweeping that, in the part of the country south of Mersey and Humber at least, only a handful of the pre-1066 landholders with estates worth more than £100 remained in possession.[38] Stenton named Colswein of Lincoln and Turchil of Warwick;[39] other men possibly of mixed blood, like Edward of Salisbury (whose mother may have been the noble Wulfwyn) and William Malet have been suggested.[40] The daughters of some Saxon lords gave a formal legitimation to the transfer of land to their Norman husbands, as did Eadgyth, daughter of Wigod of Wallingford. She married Robert d'Oilly – and their daughter, Matilda of Wallingford, married Miles Crispin from an important Norman family well-endowed in England.[41] A few Normans who had accompanied Edward the Confessor to England and had settled in the Welsh marches remained.

The change, however, took some time to complete, and this affected the way in which estates were distributed among the invaders. Here refinements have been introduced, and different interpretations have emerged. Among recent books, a full-length study by Ann Williams on *The English and the Norman Conquest* has described in detail the stages by which the transfer of great English estates was brought about after successive rebellions. King William's claim was, as the lawful successor of Edward the Confessor, to preserve ancient laws and to take nothing except by due process of law. In the first wave of redistribution he handed out some lands from the royal demesne, together with the confiscated estates of the Godwine family and the other men who had fought against the Normans at Hastings. The revolts of the earls Edwin and Morcar, a succession of risings in the north, and finally the revolt of Roger, earl of Hereford, the Anglo-Breton Ralph, earl of East Anglia, and Waltheof, earl of the east Midlands and Bamburgh, made further great properties available for distribution.[42] By the time Domesday Book was compiled the massive replacement of the 'English' in the upper ranks of the aristocracy had been completed.[43] Ann Williams shows, however, that in some regions such as Shropshire 'Englishmen were not so much dispossessed as depressed in tenurial status', and that some survived as holders of a portion of their ancestral estates. Some held lands at farm, like Aethelric, who held his manor at Marsh Gibbon from William fitz Ansculf 'in heaviness and misery'.[44] The highest rate of survival of the better men was in the western shires and the north. There was survival with suppressed status in most regions, though the extent is difficult to quantify. And among the most debatable of remaining problems are the fate of the English in the middling ranks of society, and the changes in the condition of the peasantry.

Recent work based on an analysis of Domesday Book has discussed the method by which estates were built up. So rapid a change in lordship inevitably led to confusion and uncertainty over rights. There is general agreement that two methods of land transfer were used: the first antecessorial, the handing over of the land of one or more English previous holders to a Norman baron; the second territorial, when fees were made up from lands in a particular region, granted out partly by the local divisions of hundred and wapentake within counties.[45] Such lordships were commonly based on castles; some, like the rapes of Sussex, were established very quickly on the southern coast, others were built up within a few years in the marches of Wales and the north, in the frontier regions of advancing Norman conquest and settlement. These involved much more drastic dispossession of English landholders.

The major controversy that has largely replaced the old 'English versus Norman' debate is the extent and nature of the territorial revolution. Historians with different views have supported their assertions by analysis of sections of Domesday Book. Owing to the great diversity of tenures, and the different types of material available in the various circuits of the Domesday commissioners, the different conclusions reached are hardly surprising. Among those stressing continuity, Peter Sawyer claimed that the antecessorial method of transfer was most prevalent. From the examples cited he argued that 'pre-Conquest England had fiefs very much like those of 1086'.[46] Robin Fleming, however, in a much more comprehensive analysis of the whole Domesday Book, maintained that this was only true of certain places. Her conclusion was that, after several changes of lordship in the period 1066 to 1086, one finds that from

Domesday Book's four or five thousand secular Saxon landlords in 1066, only a few more than 100 significant *antecessores* can be identified – though in some shires and certain fees, particularly in Eastern England, the organisation of pre-Conquest landholding and lordship survived the first twenty years of Norman rule.[47] In spite of some continuity. particularly on Church lands, she argues in favour of a general tenurial revolution.

A recent study of the aristocracy of Norman England by Judith Green underlines the intention of the Conqueror to make the transition orderly.[48] She examines the country by regions, showing a considerable number of English survivors in the frontier districts, particularly the north, which was 'a patchwork of regions with different histories, ethnic composition and political alignments'. Her conclusion is that the new regime was 'only a thin veneer, so that distinctive features in northern society were better able to survive'. A similar point is made by William Aird, in a valuable study of the church of Durham, that 'each of the communities which made up the region identified as the north of England also has individual historical identities'.[49]

The incompleteness of the Domesday evidence, particularly in the north of England, leaves the way open for different interpretations. David Roffe has questioned some of Fleming's conclusions about antecessorial holdings, pointing out that Domesday Book does not fully record pre-conquest patterns of overlordship. A number of Anglo-Scandinavian thegns were often tenants of a single lord, so that some of the compact lordships often regarded as Norman creations may already have existed before 1066.[50] Paul Dalton, in his regional study of Yorkshire extending over nearly a century, has argued for a greater and more rapid establishment of Norman power in Yorkshire than has usually been recognised.[51] He describes the systematic way in which William the Conqueror had set about establishing lordships based on castles that were carefully situated at strategic points. At the same time, Dalton modestly points out, his approach 'is only one of many possible approaches ... intended as a contribution to an on-going debate rather than the last word on the subject'.[52] This, indeed, admirably sums up the present-day state of many conquest studies.

Institutional change was a topic of fierce controversy in the middle years of the twentieth century, as defenders of Anglo-Saxon or Norman institutions hunted for early signs of a chancery, the use of seals, the origin of the jury, the early borough customs, various types of fortifications, the financial system and the currency. The efficiency of the Old English state was compared with that of the duchy of Normandy. Fortunately an understanding has been reached between the contestants, with the recognition that both countries were strongly centralised and exceptionally efficient, though in different ways.[53] James Campbell and Patrick Wormald in particular did much to illuminate the workings of the English government and administration;[54] R. A. Brown and David Douglas, with cross-Channel support from Lucien Musset and Jean Yver, showed that Normandy too was wealthy and by no means backward.[55] Many historians now are open to more flexible interpretations: as James Campbell wrote in considering some agents and agencies in the late Old-English state, '"probably", "perhaps" and "there are indications that" are the leitmotifs of this speculative paper'.[56]

Some of the early controversies were due to the difficulty of interpreting scanty sources. The debate on the use of seals and the existence of a chancery is one example of the way new evidence broke down old theories. As long as the only attempt at a published collection of William I's charters was the calendar in the first volume of *Regesta regum Anglo-Normannorum*, eked out with publications of individual charters in scattered sources,[57] the early ducal administration could not be studied adequately; and even the early work of French scholars was insufficiently used in English universities. After an edition of ducal charters up to 1066 appeared in 1961, Douglas was able to attack the view that the ducal administration was primitive; he calculated that up to 1066 Duke William issued or subscribed nearly the same number of writs and charters as Edward the Confessor (1042–66).[58] R. A. Brown insisted that, even allowing for the fact that (as Pierre Chaplais had shown) many charters were already authenticated by the duke, William had at least the nucleus of a chancery organisation on the eve of the conquest.[59] Marie Fauroux suggested that the equestrian seal that William used after 1066 argues for an earlier Norman seal, since no English seal showed the king as a mounted warrior.[60] Simon Keynes, on the basis of charter references to sealing made a case for the sealing of pre-1066 English diplomas.[61]

All this was tentative and suggestive. The publication of David Bates's edition of the charters of the conquest has at last provided the material for a much more precise evaluation of the evidence.[62] The collection includes many previously unknown charters; many, however, have survived only in later copies which may have been tampered with. No new examples of seals have come to light, so the subject still 'does not admit of an easy answer'.[63] After carefully examining the form and language of royal diplomas and writs in both England and Normandy after 1066, Bates decided that there could be no doubt that 'the practice of sealing diplomas continued in England over 1066', and spread in Normandy whatever previous practice there may have been. On the question of whether anything that could properly be called a chancery existed in either dominion before 1066 he is equally cautious. But he notes the marked increase in central control in England after about 1070. From 1066 to 1070 some documents were produced in Old English, and some of the staff of the English royal writing office were employed until new scribes could become more familiar with the agents and agencies alredy existing in the conquered country. After 1070 there was a sharp change: Latin became the normal language of writs, and the witnesses increasingly included individuals 'closely associated with the enactment of the king's will'.[64] His final conclusion was that, although in 1087 the time when the royal chancery would normally write the majority of writs and diplomas was in the far future, the chancery was already a significant organisation. In formal terms, he considered that its origins were primarily English. Yet 'it was staffed by men both well versed in the technicalities of writing and using literate means of government, qualities which are abundantly evident in pre-1066 Norman charters'.[65]

Some of Bates's conclusions about changes in royal government deduced from a study of the charters are reinforced by the conclusions of a number of scholars analysing Domesday Book. These too show a significant change after about 1070. In particular, Robin Fleming has examined all the hundreds of references to legal proceedings about property rights which took place as a result of the survey. They form the climax to a number of great land pleas that had taken place earlier in the reign, largely because of disputes already begun on the estates of the greatest ecclesiastical lords. Some were complaints of spoliation dating from before the conquest, others resulted from violent seizures by the Normans. King William had used traditional methods of initiating pleas by royal writ and the use of sworn inquisitions in the local shire courts, sometimes in joint sessions of several shires.[66] Because the property of Church lords was respected, in principle at least, these pleas provided continuity with pre-conquest practice. By 1085 it was clear that, in addition to pleas concerning Church lands, complaints of violent dispossession on smaller lay estates were being heard in all parts of the country. The king, claiming to be the lawful successor of King Edward and therefore pledged to uphold Edward's laws, set in motion by his writs a far wider inquest into property in every part of the kingdom. It involved numerous hearings in local hundred and wapentake as well as shire courts, and the summoning of local juries to give sworn testimony. As Robin Fleming has pointed out, 'the disruption of the Norman settlement was mitigated in crucial ways by older, native ideas about law and landholding'. About half the jurors were Englishmen from the ranks of thegns and greater freemen, who were familiar with English customs.[67] So oral testimony was brought into contact with the ideas of lordship and knightly inheritance familiar to the invaders, and oral testimony was blended with the written records provided by the greater lords through their stewards.

What emerged from the melting pot of the years of intense activity was a blend of English and Norman custom, enforceable in both the traditional local courts and in the courts of the lords of the land. It was still far from the common law of the late twelfth century, but the methods and characteristics of a common law were beginning to emerge. Moreover, the great guarantee against social disintegration was in the effective power of the king at the centre. From about 1070, when the worst of the revolts had been suppressed, and his officers had learnt how to take over the older institutions, King William began to extend the use of the royal writ in significant ways. The Anglo-Danish kings had used it chiefly to initiate proceedings which directly affected royal estates or royal rights; the new Norman king began to use it regularly to bring disputes between other individuals into the shire courts.[68] This practice did not attack the honorial courts of the greater barons where they were competent to deal with a case; Henry I made this clear early in his reign.[69] But writs were available for suits between vassals of different lords, or even to hear complaints of defect of justice. In time the honour courts withered away, but for over a century they played a significant part in the handling of claims to property. It will be interesting to see how the debate develops in the light of the most recent work. Much recent historical discussion has been about such topics as the speed of change, the contribution made by royal and seigniorial courts, and the nature of property rights. Interpretations are sufficiently different for the question, 'Was there a tenurial revolution?' to be a real one.

Notes

1 J. G. A. Pocock, *The Ancient Constitution and the Feudal Law* (Cambridge, 1957; 2nd edn, 1987), p. 228.

2 R. H. C. Davis,'The Norman Conquest', *History* 51 (1966), pp. 279–86

3 D. C. Douglas, *William the Conqueror* (London, 1964), pp. 96–8.

4 Jean Yver, 'Les premières institutions du duché de Normandie', *I Normanni è la loro espansione in Europa nell'alto medieoevo*, Centro Italiano di Studi sull'Alto Medioevo, Settimane 16 (Spoleto, 1969), pp. 299–366, at pp. 334–7.

5 J. C. Holt, '1086', in *Domesday Studies*, ed. J. C. Holt (Woodbridge, Suffolk, 1987), pp. 41–64, at pp. 42–3.

6 C. Wickham, 'The other transition: from the ancient world to feudalism', *Past and Present* 113 (1984), pp. 3–36; Chris Wickham, *Land and Power*, British School at Rome (London, 1994), pp. 7–42, at p. 33.

7 E. A. R. Brown, 'The tyranny of a construct; feudalism and historians of medieval Europe', *American Historical Review* 79 (1974), pp. 1063–88.

8 Susan Reynolds, *Fiefs and Vassals* (Oxford, 1994), p. 2.

9 *Ibid.*, pp. 342–3.

10 *Ibid.*, pp. 348–9.

11 *Speculum* 71 (1996), pp. 998–1006.

12 'The Feudal Revolution', *Past and Present* 152 (1996), pp. 6–42, 196–223, and 153 (1997), pp. 177–208.

13 T. N. Bisson, *Past and Present* 152 (1996), pp. 6–42.

14 Timothy Reuter, *Past and Present* 153 (1997), pp. 177–95.

15 Chris Wickham, *Past and Present* 153 (1997), pp. 196–208.

16 Reynolds, *Fiefs and Vassals*, p. 350.

17 See above, p. 75.

18 F. Cheyette, review of Reynolds, *Fiefs and Vassals*, in *Speculum* 71 (1996), p. 1006.
19 Holt, '1086', p. 41. For Martin Wright and Blackstone, see above, pp. 49–50.
20 Quoted from F. M. Stenton, *The First Century of English Feudalism, 1066–1166*, 2nd edn (Oxford, 1961), p. 112.
21 Holt, '1086', pp. 55–7.
22 *Ibid.*, pp. 57–9.
23 E. M. Hallam, *Domesday Book through Nine Centuries* (London, 1986), pp. 32–5; V. H. Galbraith, *Domesday Book: Its Place in Administrative History* (Oxford, 1974), pp. 100–123.
24 Hallam, *Domesday Book*, p. 24; H. B. Clarke, 'The Domesday Satellites', in *Domesday Book: a Reassessment*, ed. P. Sawyer (London, 1985), pp. 50–70, at p. 56.
25 J. A. Green, *The Aristocracy of Norman England* (Cambridge, 1997), pp. 217–18.
26 *The Cartulary of Lilleshall Abbey*, ed. Una Rees, Shropshire Archaeological and Historical Society (1997), p. 165, no. 324.
27 Lindy Grant, *Abbot Suger of St Denis* (London and New York, 1998), p. 14.
28 J. O. Prestwich, 'War and finance in the Anglo-Norman state', *TRHS*, 5th ser., 4 (1954), pp. 19–43; M. Strickland, ed., *Anglo-Norman Warfare* (repr. Woodbridge, Suffolk, 1992), pp. 59–83. See also M. Chibnall, 'Mercenaries and the *familia regis* under Henry I', *History* 62 (1977), pp. 15–23; Strickland, *Anglo-Norman Warfare*, pp. 84–92.
29 Richard fitz Nigel, *Dialogus de Scaccario*, ed. Charles Johnson, corr. F. E. L. Carter and D. E. Greenway OMT (Oxford, 1983), pp. 1–2.
30 J. O. Prestwich, 'The military household of the Norman kings', *English Historical Review* 96 (1981), pp. 1–37; Strickland, *Anglo-Norman Warfare*, pp. 93–127.
31 Georges Duby, 'Au XIIᵉ les jeunes dans la société aristocratique dans la France du nord-ouest', *Annales: Économies, Société, Civilisation* trans. Cynthia Postan as 'Youth in aristocratic society', in *The Chivalrous Society* (London, 1977), pp. 112–22.
32 R. A. Brown, 'The status of the Norman knight', *War and Government* in the *Middle Ages*, eds J. Gillingham and J. C. Holt (Woodbridge, Suffolk, 1984), pp. 18–32; Strickland, *Anglo-Norman Warfare*, pp. 128–42, which questions the interpretation of S. Harvey in 'The knight and the knight's fee in England', *Past and Present* 49 (1970), p. 15.
33 Strickland, *Anglo-Norman Warfare*.
34 The Proceedings of the Conferences were published by Boydell, first as *Proceedings of the Battle Conference in Anglo-Norman Studies* from 1979–82, and since 1983 as *Anglo-Norman Studies*; vols 1–10 were edited by R. A. Brown, 11–15 by M. Chibnall, and from 16 onwards by C. Harper-Bill.
35 The *Haskins Society Journal* publishes selected papers from these conferences.
36 Papers (in French) read at these conferences are published by the University of Caen and edited by P. Bouet and F. Neveux.
37 The view of C. W. C. Oman on the very primitive tactics of the Norman armies has been demolished by numerous studies of the tactical skill of the

armies; see R. A. Brown, 'The battle of Hastings', *Anglo-Norman Studies* 3
(1951), pp. 1–21; Strickland, *Anglo-Norman Warfare*, pp. 161–81; J.
Gillingham, 'William the Bastard at war', *Studies in Medieval History
presented to R. Allen Brown*, eds C. Harper-Bill, C. Holdsworth and J.
Nelson (Woodbridge, Suffolk, 1989), pp. 141–58; Strickland, *Anglo-Norman
Warfare*, pp. 143–60; I. Peirce, 'Arms, armour and warfare in the eleventh
century', *Anglo-Norman Studies* 10 (1987), pp. 237–58; and in general,
Stephen Morillo, *Warfare under the Anglo-Norman Kings, 1066–1135*
(Woodbridge, Suffolk, 1994), esp. pp. 136–79. On fortifications and the
purpose of castles being both military and residential, see R. Allen Brown,
'The castles of the Conquest', *Domesday Book Studies*, eds A. Williams and
R. W. H. Erskine (London, 1987), pp. 65–74; R. A. Brown, *English Castles*
(2nd edn, London, 1976); N. J. G. Pounds, *The Medieval Castle in England
and Wales: A Social and Political History* (Cambridge, 1990). On logistics,
see B. S. Bachrach, 'Some observations on the military administration of the
Norman Conquest', *Anglo-Norman Studies* 8 (1985), pp. 1–26; E. M. C. van
Houts, 'The ship list of William the Conqueror', *Anglo-Norman Studies* 10
(1987), pp. 159–84; C. Gillmor, 'Naval logistics and the cross-Channel,
operation', *Anglo-Norman Studies* 7 (1984), pp. 105–31.
38 Green, *Aristocracy*, pp. 96–7.
39 F. M. Stenton, 'English families and the Norman Conquest', *TRHS*, 4th ser.,
26 (1944), pp. 1–12.
40 Green, *Aristocracy*, pp. 96–7; Ann Williams, *The English and the Norman
Conquest* (Woodbridge, Suffolk, 1995), ch. 4.
41 Green, *Aristocracy*, pp. 61, 77; Eleanor Searle, 'Women and the legitimiza-
tion of succession at the Norman Conquest', *Anglo-Norman Studies* 3
(1981), pp. 159–70.
42 Williams, *The English*, chs 2, 3.
43 *Ibid.*, p. 98.
44 *Ibid.*, pp. 89, 79.
45 R. Fleming, *Kings and Lords in Conquest England* (Cambrdge, 1991), pp.
122–58.
46 P. Sawyer, '1066–1086: a tenurial revolution?', in his *Domesday Book: A
Reassessment?* (London, 1985), pp. 75–85, at pp. 76–8.
47 Fleming, *Kings and Lords*, pp. 109–14.
48 Green, *Aristocracy*, pp. 49–50.
49 *Ibid.*, pp. 124–5; William M. Aird, *St Cuthbert and the Normans*
(Woodbridge, Suffolk, 1998), pp. 270–1.
50 D. Roffe, 'From thegnage to barony: sake and soke, title and tenants-in-
chief', *Anglo-Norman Studies* 12(1990), pp. 157–76, at p. 169.
51 Paul Dalton, *Conquest, Anarchy and Lordship. Yorkshire, 1066–1154*
(Cambridge, 1994), pp. 72–3.
52 *Ibid.*, p. 22.
53 See David Bates, *Normandy before 1066* (London and New York, 1982); M.
Chibnall, *Anglo-Norman England 1066–1166* (Oxford, 1986), esp. pp.
105–6; J. Le Patourel, *The Norman Empire* (Oxford, 1976).
54 J. Campbell, *Essays in Anglo-Saxon History* (London, 1986); J. Campbell,
'The late Anglo-Saxon state: a maximum view', *Proceedings of the British*

Academy 87 (1995), pp. 39–65; P. Wormald, '*Laga Eadwardi*: the *Textus Roffensis* and its context', *Anglo-Norman Studies* 17 (1995), pp. 243–66; P. Wormald, *The Making of the English Law: King Alfred to the Norman Conquest* (Oxford, forthcoming).

55 D. C. Douglas, *William the Conqueror* (London, 1964); R. Allen Brown, *The Normans and the Norman Conquest* (2nd edn, Woodbridge, Suffolk, 1985); J. Yver, 'Les premières institutions' (Spoleto, 1969); L. Musset, 'Gouvernés et gouvernants dans le monde scandinave et dans le monde normand', *Recueils de la Société Jean Bodin* 23 (Brussels, 1968).

56 James Campbell, 'Some agents and agencies of the late Anglo-Saxon state', in *Domesday Studies*, ed. J. C. Holt (Woodbridge, Suffolk, 1987), pp. 201–18, at p. 218.

57 *Regesta Regum Anglo-Normannorum, 1066–1154*, 4 vols, vol. 1, ed. H. W. C. Davis (Oxford, 1913).

58 Douglas, *William the Conqueror*, p. 11.

59 R. A. Brown, 'Some observations on Norman and Anglo-Norman charters', in *Tradition and Change*, ed. D. Greenway, C. Holdsworth, J. Sayers (Cambridge, 1985), pp. 145–63.

60 *Recueil des actes des ducs de Normandie de 911 à 1066*, ed. Marie Fauroux, Mémoires de la Société des Antiquaires de Normandie 36 (Caen, 1961), pp. 46–7.

61 Simon Keynes, 'Regenbald the Chancellor (*sic*)', *Anglo-Norman Studies* 10 (1988), pp. 185–222, at p. 216.

62 *Regesta Regum Anglo-Normannorum, 1066–1087*, ed. David Bates (Oxford, 1998).

63 *Ibid.*, p. 103.

64 *Ibid.*, pp. 106–8.

65 *Ibid.*, p. 108.

66 R. Fleming, 'Oral testimony and the Domesday inquest', *Anglo-Norman Studies* 17 (1995), pp. 101–22.

67 Robin Fleming, *Domesday Book and the Law* (Cambridge, 1998), p. 83; this important new study prints and analyses all the disputes. C. P. Lewis, 'The Domesday jurors', *Haskins Society Journal* 5 (1993), pp. 17–29.

68 Fleming, 'Oral testimony', pp. 112–17.

69 *Regesta Regum Anglo-Normannorum, 1066–1154*, eds C. Johnson, H. A. Cronne and H. W. C. Davis (Oxford, 1956), 2, no. 892.

7

The later twentieth century: law and the family

We must protest against the common assumption that the English law of later times must in some sort be a mixture, or a compound of two old national laws.

F. W. Maitland

Law has always had a prominent place in the debate on the conquest, with property law at its heart. It has occupied the attention of scholars in England, France and America, working on many different materials. The Anglo-Saxon law codes were far from comprehensive, and none exist for the reigns of Cnut and Edward the Confessor.[1] Norman customs were not written down until the end of the twelfth century.[2] Some collections of materials alleged to be earlier laws, which were produced in England after the conquest, are fanciful, and even the *Leges Henrici Primi* and the so-called *Quadripartitus* are speculative collections of very variable value.[3] Moreover, the English common law which was slowly emerging was case law, not dependent on clearly defined legislation. The interests of legal historians such as Spelman and Hale had been in the common law as it existed in the seventeenth century, and they had not had the information necessary to trace particular customs to their source. So from an early date there has been ample material for the debates of scholars.

The influence of French historians began to be felt early in the twentieth century, and they led rapidly to studies of the family. After J. Généstal, of the University of Caen, published his seminal work on *Le parage normand*,[4] Caen became an active centre for the study of 'droit', which included economics as well as law, and so placed the subject in its social context. Généstal's mantle fell on Jean Yver, who pushed the history of family law and inheritance back from the thirteenth century, when the customs were first written down, into the mid-eleventh century.[5] Ideas were freely exchanged in regular meetings of regional societies concerned with the history of 'droit', and these drew in some English scholars. John Le Patourel was active in relating Norman custom to work on England after the conquest.[6] Later a substantial contribution came from an American scholar, Emily Zack Tabuteau.[7] This new work widened the scope of studies of property, tenure and lordship that were of fundamental importance in the debate on the consequences of the Norman Conquest.

In July 1995, a symposium met in Cambridge to celebrate the centenary of Pollock and Maitland's *History of English Law*,[8] which J. H. Round had first welcomed as a 'work which superseded all that went before it'.[9] After a hundred years an impressive amount of Maitland's work had survived the critical examination of generations of scholars; but the time had come for a comprehensive review. The symposium looked at changes in the history of law since Maitland's day; and, though it showed ways in which Maitland's work needed to be supplemented and corrected, it brought out the remarkable penetration and suggestiveness of Maitland's judgements. It showed too that law was central to the changes in both government and social structures. Since Maitland's work has worn better than that of any other historian of the late nineteenth century, this scholarly assessment in particularly valuable.

Maitland was unfortunately less interested in the period between Domesday Book and the treatise known as Glanville than in the history of law from the time of Henry II onwards. Domesday Book, the subject of the Oxford lectures that gave rise to *Domesday Book and Beyond*, was the chief exception in the earlier period. Yet even here he broke off his investigation of that difficult source (not, perhaps, entirely without relief) because he modestly insisted that Round, also occupied with the subject, would do it better.[10] At least, though his work in the field of Anglo-Norman law was tentative, he indicated some of the areas to be developed, and these were considered by John Hudson in his contribution to the symposium.[11] The first was language: how to use modern characterisations, and hence language, when writing about medieval law.[12] Words such as 'property/ownership' and 'rights' carry a great deal of modern mental baggage and our use of them can lead to vagueness and confusion. What Maitland wrote of the thirteenth century shows that he was well aware of the difficulty of expressing in legal terms exactly what property and tenure meant in the two centuries following the conquest. Contemporary historians are still grappling with the problems, and some of the apparent conflicts or disagreements arise from their attempts to explain in the language of the present day what the words meant when they were first used.

A second area of development, in Hudson's analysis, is the scope of the law's domain.[13] While Maitland was aware of some of the many ways in which courts could be used, later legal historians have extended their range still further, to take in disputes from the time of their first origin, as well as the different methods of dispute settlement. The use of power too has been brought into the debate; the sources considered have sometimes included literary accounts of trials, though such accounts are most frequently concerned with treason.[14]

The third topic of considerable later interest has been the place of the Norman Conquest in the development of Anglo-Norman law. It is one of the most fundamental questions on the effects of the conquest, being bound up equally with customary law and with courts and institutions. Maitland had referred to 'the hundred forces which play upon our legal history' and had insisted that English law as it developed was not just a compound of two old national laws.[15] He also showed flashes of insight on the nature of the common law as it finally emerged. 'We can not', he wrote, 'as continental writers do, treat feudal law as distinct from the ordinary law of the land'.[16] At the same time he wrote in more precise detail of continuity rather than change over the period of the conquest. He suggested that there were some analogies between socage and the various tenures in Domesday Book described as 'holding freely', and suggested that some thegnages at least may have re-emerged as serjeanties.[17] On commendation and homage he observed, 'The Normans saw their homage in the English commendation. The fidelity of the thegn is not regarded as a debt incurred by the receipt of land'.[18] So on balance Hudson is justified in claiming with Brunner that Maitland underestimated Norman influence after 1066, adding that he wrote little about lords' courts.[19]

These limitations were caused partly by the lack of available sources. The past hundred years have enriched the historian in two ways. First, thousands of charters illustrating in detail the relations between lords and men, and the pleadings taking place in honorial and other courts, have been published. Second, the use of computer technology has made possible a much quicker and more nuanced analysis of formulae and the witness lists to charters. It is now easier to see the gradual change over a period of about a century; and the kind of change that produces case law is normally gradual. It is also possible sometimes to detect whether the change was hastened at any particular time.

Even in the period before the Second World War, Stenton had pointed out the importance of the honour courts in handling a considerable share of land litigation, particularly in the first half of the twelfth century.[20] He described the workings of the honour with its centre and court at the *caput honoris*, often a castle or at least a fortified residence of the lord. He did not see the honour as a closed unit (as his critics have sometimes alleged), but showed that 'the lord was confronted with a variety of administrative and judicial duties similar to those which fell upon the king himself'.[21] From the first the court had not been competent to settle cases between litigants who were not both his vassals, and many barons held lands of several lords; there were cases which might have to be carried to the king's court, as Henry I had recognised.[22] Many other cases were settled satisfactorily in the court of a lord.

S. F. C. Milsom, examining the 'legal framework of English feudalism' appreciated and developed Stenton's meaning.[23] In the century after the conquest there were some generally accepted customs of inheritance, and normally when a tenant died his lord would follow the customs and accept his 'heir'. This, however, would be simply a decision taken on a particular occasion. As the king's writ of right was introduced more and more frequently from the reign of Henry II, it was 'working in the same direction as the established customs of the lord's court, enforcing them in particular cases'. But 'so long as there was only the lord's court, the canons of inheritance, however clearly settled and however consistently followed, were criteria for making a choice. They were not rules of law conferring an abstract right on the heir, but customs about whom the lord's court should choose'. The great change was in the growth of rules of law. The change could sometimes be seen in its effects, for instance, on warranty.[24] By taking homage the lord warranted the man whom he had admitted as heir to a tenement. But if a rival heir, claiming a greater right, won his case, the warranty would carry only a right to compensation, not the 'conclusive title to the tenement'. Looking at the fundamental changes, Milsom wrote, 'Conceptual changes are never visible as they proceed .... As to the practical changes, the realistic question is whether anybody could ever see what was happening clearly enough to resist it, and this turns upon how fast it happened'.[25]

Milsom approached the whole question of property rights as a lawyer, and expected to be criticised by historians; they have not been slow to take up the challenge.[26] This does not, however, invalidate his arguments. He provided the legal framework within which historians might follow and understand the gradual changes taking place, and in this way he enriched the debate by approaching it from the angle of a different discipline. Indeed, much historical writing of the past three decades has been concerned with reviewing earlier controversies which had resulted from seeing the changes after the conquest as unduly sudden or inevitable, or from emphasising one period rather than another. To write of the importance of the writ of right (or other writs) in the reign of Henry II does not necessarily imply that there were no precedents in the time of Henry I. Opinions may well differ on the most significant points in a gradual change; but the suggestion that certain legal or institutional changes were due to the Norman Conquest is more likely to mean that they resulted from the slow interaction of Norman and English customs in a new situation, than that they sprang from the importation of Norman practices.

Among the legal changes, the customs governing inheritance are a valuable illustration of the way in which changes occured after 1066 on both sides of the Channel. By the mid-eleventh century, family custom – as it developed in Normandy – was rapidly moving towards the complicated arrangements of '*parage*'. *Parage* customs maintained the integrity of the patrimony and gave some prominence to the first-born, without neglecting the claims of other members of the family. Well before the conquest the basic customary division between patrimony and acquisitions had become firmly established in Normandy.[27] Historians have become increasingly aware of this. Between 1982 and 1985 J. C. Holt gave a series of presidential addresses to the Royal Historical Society on the subject of 'Feudal society and the family in early Medieval England'.[28] These summed up the progress of the debate, and clarified the issues. He pointed to the different attitudes to kinship and lordship that prevailed in Anglo-Saxon England and ducal Normandy, in both of which the family was important. In England, social conventions 'allowed, even required, the testamentary distribution of land throughout the kin'. In Normandy, a different convention required some provision to be made for younger sons, provided the patrimony was not permanently alienated.[29] Their share might be modest; in a large family it sometimes amounted to no more than a horse and armour with which to earn a living in the household troops of some lord. But the custom which respected hereditary right did not necessarily require primogeniture. Chattels were available for testamentary disposition.

So the conquest 'involved not simply the replacement of one aristocracy by another, but also the replacement of one set of family relationships by another'.[30] Moreover, the military character of the conquest, which led to the acquisition of estates so large that often the acquisitions outstripped the patrimony in size, led at first to greater freedom in dividing up an inheritance; the eldest son might prefer the acquisitions to the patrimony. Once the supply of new lands dried up, the rights of the first-born assumed a greater importance. Primogeniture became at first a preferred option, then a fixed custom. In Normandy, on the other hand, the claims of the eldest son were respected in the developed *parage* customs, which allowed the first-born to inherit the patrimony. Younger sons received some share from his hands, and did homage to him (though after several generations their land reverted to the patrimony). In England customs changed in a different way. The rule that 'no man can be lord and heir' became established, and there was no question of a younger son (who might outlive the elder and become the next heir) performing homage. The position of women in the family was gradually being modified at the same time.

Women were by no means without property rights.[31] Customs of dower from their own family and dowry from their husband gave them some entitlement to property, both for charitable giving and to secure them from destitution in widowhood. Even though, once married, they might require their husband's consent to alienate property, they were never in the unfortunate position of Victorian women before the passing of the first Married Women's Property Act. Moreover, they could inherit the family patrimony when male heirs failed. So they were desirable partners in marriage. This led Holt to suggest the reason for what appears to be a deliberate change in the inheritance rights of women noted by Stenton.

Stenton had seen the reference in a private charter to a *statutum decretum* agreed in one of Henry I's courts late in his reign. One of the very rare deliberate rulings on property law in this period, it appeared to define the rights of daughters and proposed that, when male heirs failed, the property should be divided equally between the daughters.[32] Holt suggested that this had not been the custom in either Normandy or England for some decades after the conquest. During that period the eldest daughter had inherited the whole property and in Normandy her sisters (with their husbands) had held their share from her. This was to become the accepted *parage* custom in Normandy and France, whereas division between heiresses was to prevail in England. Holt plausibly suggested that the magnates meeting in Henry I's court had an interest in securing as many potential heiresses as possible to be the wives of portionless younger sons. It was significant that the change was made just when the sources of new lands to be won as acquisitions were drying up.[33] This is an illustration of the slow working-out of changes resulting from the conquest, which was characteristic of the first century of Anglo-Norman England. Holt's interpretation has been questioned by Judith Green, who suggests that the change to division between heiresses was more gradual and took some time from 1130 to 1180 to become normal.[34] This would not, however, exclude the possibility that Henry I's court had voiced a general principle that was gradually applied more widely.

Since the mid-twentieth century, womens' studies have assumed an increasingly important place in historical writing. An upsurge of interest in the history of women has led to the introduction in many universities of sub-departments devoted to the subject. In a reaction to the tunnel vision sometimes caused by excessive concentration on women to the exclusion of men, this is becoming widened into gender studies. In England only a few historians in the early part of the century had discussed the place of women in society, although a few research endowments had come into existence to encourage work on questions related to women. Eileen Power was first drawn into research in women's history as a holder of the Shaw studentship at the London School of Economics, which (from 1911) was for women only.[35] Because a subject related to the position of women was required, she began work on medieval nunneries, while developing her wider interests in literary and cultural history. Her most mature later work was in more general social and economic history. In any case, she had no special concern with the Norman Conquest.[36] It was left to Doris Stenton to give prominence to the influence of the conquest on the position of English women.

Doris Stenton was essentially a legal historian, and in her book on *The English Woman in History* she investigated the legal position of women before and after the conquest, making particular use of Anglo-Saxon wills and the post-conquest evidence put together by Maitland.[37] The weakness of her approach was its unilinear character and its sweeping generalisations which were cited in general textbooks without regard even for the modifications she herself described. Maitland had suggested that a woman who was a spinster or a widow was a fully competent person 'for all the purposes of private law, and could sue and be sued, make feoffments and seal bonds just as a man could'.[38] Doris Stenton cited the rights specified by Maitland, but concluded that 'in a military society it was inevitable that those who could not fight should take second place to those who fought'.[39] In her view, men and women in Anglo-Saxon society had lived on terms of 'rough equality', and the conquest ultimately led to a deterioration in the position of women. This general conclusion held the field for some time. Even Henry Loyn, in a well-balanced book on *England and the Norman Conquest* took the line that the Normans introduced a harsh world, and that 'the legal position of women was less favourable under the Normans than under the Anglo-Saxons. On the critical questions of inheritance and dower the world of the Anglo-Norman aristocrats was very much a man's world'.[40]

Such a view was gradually modified under the influence of work on family history. J. C. Holt's seminal work on the family and the Norman Conquest showed the gradual changes resulting from the interaction of slowly developing custom on both sides of the Channel, and the influence of royal power.[41] Important as the sudden acquisition of huge new patrimonies by the invading aristocracy undoubtedly was, the most significant changes took over half a century to become evident. By the time of Henry II the position of noble women, though different, was not simply worse. Their rights as heirs in certain circumstances, and as transmitters of property to their direct descendants in preference to collaterals, were clearly recognised. Among those working on the position of women, Marc A. Meyer emphasised the influence of the Church together with the family to offer a more nuanced interpretation of the eleventh-century changes.[42] He noted that even a cursory reading of the early English penitentials and law codes

> dispels the myth of 'rough equality' before the conquest. The ability of women to leave property was governed by family customs of inheritance, and only chattels, not land, could be freely bequeathed. Moreover after no less than before the conquest women could, by observing the correct forms, give or sell land to a religious house and inherit it if there was no male heir. And the members of the highest aristocracy, above all royal ladies, had powers much greater than those of the rank and file.

Meyer cited Domesday statistics for the amount of land held by women in 1066, and found that it amounted to no more than five per cent of the recorded hidage, and of that hidage between eighty and eighty-five per cent was in the hands of eight women of very high status.[43] None of these studies attempted to analyse conditions in the lowest ranks. Peasant inheritance customs were quite another matter. They varied all over the country, and were not influenced by ability to participate in war; women were as capable as men of performing even the most arduous agricultural tasks.

The second most recent influence has been the mushroom growth of women's studies. Although the subject has sometimes been vitiated by rampant feminism, at its best – as, for example, in the work of Pauline Stafford – it has made a useful contribution to the study of social and legal history, and incidentally to consideration of the effects of the Norman Conquest. Stafford attacked all approaches to the subject based on the romantic view of a Golden Age for women in pre-conquest England, which had appeared in many earlier writings.[44] As she pointed out, 'in the nineteenth century the "Golden Age" of high status Germanic women and the Norman Yoke on Anglo-Saxon liberties' had become ideal partners. Various writers from Kemble in 1849 to E. W. Williams in 1975 had seen Anglo-Saxon England as 'a Golden Age variously of women's domestication, women's legal emancipation, women's education, and women's sexual liberation'.[45] None of these attitudes would stand up to critical investigation. She argued against the use of 1066 as a turning-point, because for noble women in particular the legal situation both before and after the conquest was flexible, and was subject in various ways to royal interference.

> The practices of family inheritance and royal power, which are seen as critical to the framework of women's lives, span that divide. So too do movements of ecclesiastical reform and economic growth .... We need a new periodisation covering the late-ninth to the mid-twelfth century to explore a common range of factors.[46]

She questioned the historical validity of attempting to treat *all* women as a group, and the vagueness of such terms as 'high status'. Her determination to look at the eleventh century in its own terms and not, as so many had done in the past, from the angle of current political concerns, is characteristic of much that is best in present-day studies of the position of women. The interplay of flexible family custom and royal power in particular circumstances in different regions is now a central concern. In a Harvard colloquium on the general theme of 'Cultures of Power', Georges Duby contributed a clearly-focused paper on 'Women and power'.[47]

Because of the wide range of the subject, and the different position of aristocratic ladies in Germany and the kingdom of France, he asked the specific question, 'To what extent and in what ways did ladies, the wives of the aristocracy in northern France from 1050 to 1235 take part in the power of command and of punishment?' He made the important distinction between the power a woman could exercise in private, as head of a household (including administrative officers and estate managers no less than family) over which she ruled, and public power, which she might exercise only as representative of her husband when he was absent, or as a widow acting for a young son. Even then, she might overstep the bounds of what was conventionally acceptable if she acted 'in a masculine way'. Region and rank, no less than legal and moral considerations, have to be borne in mind in writing of women and the Norman Conquest.

It is not surprising, in view of the limited material available for studying the place of women in the eleventh and twelfth centuries, that much has been written about queens. From Emma of Normandy to Eleanor of Aquitaine they brought a wide range of experience and a variety of talents to the duties of queen-consort. There were no reigning queens, as the bid of the Empress Matilda for the English crown just failed, though she succeeded in passing it on to her son Henry. In the turbulent eleventh century, with its changes of dynasty from English to Scandinavian and finally to Norman, it would be difficult to generalise about the power of queens; and the same, to a lesser degree, is true of the twelfth. Clearly queens had duties extending some way beyond the traditional sphere of woman's power in ruling her household. The queens were for the most part forceful individuals, and many had experience of conditions in other countries. Emma was Norman, Edith came from the Scandinavian aristocracy settled in England, Matilda I was Flemish and French, Matilda II joined the line of the kings of Wessex with that of the kings of Scots, Matilda III was from Boulogne, the Empress Matilda had been queen-consort in Germany, Adeliza was Lotharingian, and Eleanor of Aquitaine had been queen of France before marrying the Angevin Henry II. How they used their experience in the context of English queenship depended in part at least on the character and adaptability of each of them.

Certain rights and duties contributed to queenship both

before and after 1066. The position of both Emma and Edith has been analysed in detail by Pauline Stafford.[48] Her book provides a useful basis for future discussion, though the succession disputes of the eleventh century, complicated by Danish custom, make it almost impossible to do more than indicate the various factors contributing to the position of the queen, and the conflicting views about it. As far as her control of a household and the holding of landed property go, some things are clear throughout the tenth and eleventh centuries. The queen had her own household, which was at times separate from, at others part of, the larger one. The exceptional amount of evidence in Domesday Book for Queen Edith's lands and her seventy to eighty servants does not, however, show how far this was unusual.[49] Stafford points out that her lands were 'both the patrimonial lands of a ruling family and the extended inheritance of a century and a half of kingdom building'.[50] Later history shows the survival of certain lands as traditionally the queen's dower. On balance, the conquest seems not to have caused a sharp change.

The succession question is still more complicated because of the mid-eleventh-century turmoil. Where the king had sons, or at least male heirs, the question was usually which of several brothers or grandsons had the greater right. There was no precedent in the period between 915 and 1066 for any claim to the throne by a woman or through a woman.[51] William the Conqueror, however, made his claim obliquely through his great-aunt, Emma of Normandy, mother of Edward the Confessor by her first marriage with King Æthelred. This may have been a precedent for Henry I to assert the right of his only surviving legitimate child, the Empress Matilda, to inherit as his heir. Norman family law, however, which allowed daughters to succeed when male heirs failed, could have played a part.[52] Designation of an heir among the heirs-presumptive in a family possibly gained a little ground in the period of greatest uncertainty, when Emma's sons by her two husbands were possible heirs, and Scandinavian customs further confused the issue.[53] Emma at the height of her power certainly did her best to exert some influence on the succession, and Edith may have wished to do so. The evidence does not permit the assertion that a queen had a clear right to any share in designating her husband's successor. And there is no doubt that, whatever Edith may have wished, she had no such right after the conquest.

Debates on the succession question have been more in terms of the exact line of descent that ought to prevail among male claimants, the place of the Church in making a king, and the complication of combining rule in both the duchy of Normandy and the kingdom of England, than in terms of designation.[54] Rules of inheritance were hardening in the royal family no less than in the families of the nobility, but they were not yet firmly established. And there is no evidence that the queen had ever had even the limited power of assisting in designation that Emma tried to exercise, and that Edith would like to have exercised if she could. She appears to have accepted William's succession, thereby securing a substantial part of her lands, but she had no effective share in confirming the right he claimed to the throne.

The position of the Church, on the other hand, certainly became important: William the Conqueror set a precedent by not assuming the royal title or issuing charters until he had been duly crowned. His choice was carefully made, as William of Poitiers, who knew him personally and wrote within ten years of the coronation, clearly indicated by his own careful use of the titles 'duke' before and 'king' after the ceremony.[55] Later kings dated their reigns from the time of their coronation, and issued no charters as king until they had been crowned.[56] But partly by chance no eldest son succeeded to the throne for over a hundred years, and the questionable rights of brothers led to some instability. The Conqueror's eldest son, Robert Curthose, was a disgraced rebel when his father died, but had already been accepted as duke of Normandy. He retained that title for a time after both his younger brothers, William Rufus and Henry I, had gained the English throne.[57]

This chance series of events left open the question of what rules, if any, were thought to exist for the union of both England and Normandy in the hands of one man: whether *parage* customs played any part, or whether the fact that rule in England was royal created a completely new situation in which the division of the whole inheritance was undesirable. If any general consensus has emerged, it is that claims of many kinds were made on a number of grounds for a situation without precedent; and that the way was open for force, legitimised by Church approval, to determine the outcome of any new succession. Some useful precedents were established: Matilda's long struggle made it clear that a female heir could transmit the crown, though leaving open the question of whether she could actually wear it if a rival had seized it with the blessing of the Church. At least, by successfully preventing Stephen's sons from ousting her son Henry, she established a presumption in favour of female succession that was accepted without serious question four hundred years later.[58] The loss of Normandy in 1204 radically changed the situation. Clear rules of royal succession were not, however, firmly established until the thirteenth century.

Some of the duties that fell to the queen were direct consequences of the conquest, which combined scattered territories in the hands of the kings. Earlier queens had certainly exercised royal powers as regents for underage sons or as widows. There was a tradition in Denmark of appointing members of the royal family as regents: Cnut made use of his kinsfolk, including his wife, in governing his vast realm.[59] His nephew Hakon and his wife Ælfgyfu of Northampton, with their son Swein, had acted as regents in Norway. In Normandy there was a very well-established practice of using members of the ducal family in government.[60] Almost all the earliest counts were related to the duke.[61] The question of the use of regents is bound up with a debate on the origins of the justiciarship. Here David Bates argued against the view of Francis West that there was an 'absence of any settled system of regency or formal office'.[62] He maintained that 'in England as in Normandy one member of the king/duke's family could supply an authority which was regarded as equivalent of his own'. This kind of regency was exercised by William's queen, Matilda, in Normandy until the later 1070s at times when he was out of the duchy; by Henry I's wife Matilda until her death in 1118 and thereafter for two years by his son William; by Henry II's wife Eleanor in England (sometimes with his eldest son Henry) until 1173. Governmental changes resulting from administrative developments and the emergence of 'the Angevin justiciarship, with the regency regularly devolving on the head of the exchequer' gradually replaced the earlier practice of using members of the royal family as regents.[63] Even those who might hesitate to accept this view in its entirety cannot deny that, as long as the kings used members of the royal family as regents, queens were among the first to be so employed.

How this relates to the general nature of 'queenship' is another matter. Queenship as a concept now receives some prominence in women's history. If any valid conclusions for the eleventh and twelfth centuries have emerged, they would seem to be that there was continuity in some things, particularly in the period from the mid-eleventh century until well into the reign of Henry II, but that a marked change occured at about the same time as changes already noted in administrative development and family law. Even within this period the activities of the queen depended to some extent on character: Henry I's second wife Adeliza took little direct part in royal government.[64] In the very long term some duties normally fell to all queens in Western society: most acted as intercessors with their husbands on behalf of petitioners; all exercised the kind of patronage of religious houses and other charitable institutions expected of royal ladies; all distributed rewards to the members of their household and alms to the poor.[65] The topic has gained by being examined critically in relation to the queen's position as wife, widow and mother, and to the different political circumstances in which each queen had to act.

Notes

1 Translations of some of the most important documents are printed in *English Historical Documents, c.500–1042*, ed. Dorothy Whitelock (London, 1955).

2 *Le très ancien coutumier de Normandie*, ed. E. J. Tardif (Rouen, 1881).

3 The *Leges Henrici primi* have been published by L. J. Downer (Oxford, 1972). The so-called *Quadripartitus* is discussed by Patrick Wormald, 'Quadripartitus', in *Law and Government in Medieval England and Normandy: Essays in honour of Sir James Holt*, eds George Garnett and John Hudson (Cambridge, 1994), pp. 111–47. See also Richard Sharpe, 'The prefaces to *Quadripartitus*' in the same volume, pp. 148–72.

4 R. Génestal, *Le parage normand* (Caen, 1911).

5 J. Yver, 'Les premières institutions du duché de Normandie', *I Normanni è la loro espansione in Europa nell'alto medioevo*, Centro Italiano di Studi sull'Alto Medioevo, Settimane 16 (Spoleto, 1969), pp. 299–366.

6 J. Le Patourel, *The Norman Empire* (Oxford, 1976).

7 Emily Zack Tabuteau, *Transfers of Property in Eleventh-Century Norman Law* (Chapel Hill, North Carolina, and London, 1988).

8 *The History of English Law. Centenary Essays on 'Pollock and Maitland'*, ed. John Hudson, British Academy (Oxford, 1996).
9 Cited in *ibid.*, Preface, p. ix.
10 *The Letters of Frederick William Maitland*, ed. C. H. S. Fifoot, Selden Society (London, 1965), p. 106 and n. 3.
11 John Hudson, 'Maitland and Anglo-Norman law', in *Centenary Essays* ed. Hudson, pp. 21–46.
12 *Ibid.*, pp. 32–4.
13 *Ibid.*, pp. 34–9.
14 See, for example, Paul Hyams, 'Henry II and Ganelon', *Syracuse Scholar* 4 (1983), pp. 22–35.
15 F. Pollock and F. W. Maitland, *The History of English Law before the Time of Edward I*, 2 vols (Cambridge, 1896; 2nd edn, with introduction by S. F. C. Milsom, 1968), 1, p. 80.
16 Pollock and Maitland, *History of English Law*, 1, p. 235.
17 Hudson, 'Maitland and Anglo-Norman law', pp. 43–4. Pollock and Maitland, *History of English Law*, 1, p. 279; see also J. Campbell, 'Some agents and agencies of the late Anglo-Saxon state', in *Domesday Studies*, ed. J. C. Holt, pp. 201–18, at pp. 210–12; R. R. Darlington, in the *Victoria History of the County of Wiltshire*, 1, pp. 77–8.
18 Pollock and Maitland, *History of English Law*, 1, p. 294.
19 Hudson, 'Maitland and Anglo-Norman law', p. 39.
20 F. M. Stenton, *The First Century of English Feudalism, 1066–1166* (Oxford, 1932; 2nd edn, 1961), pp. 44–5.
21 *Ibid.*, pp. 63–5.
22 Henry I's order for the holding of courts, printed in W. Stubbs, *Select Charters*, 9th edn, revd H. W. C. Davis (Oxford, 1913), p. 122.
23 S. F. C. Milsom, *The Legal Framework of English Feudalism* (Cambridge, 1976), pp. 180–5.
24 Milsom, *Legal Framework*, p. 182.
25 *Ibid.*, p. 185.
26 There is an appreciative but critical review by Paul Hyams, *English Historical Review* 93 (1978), pp. 856–61; see also J. G. H. Hudson, 'Milsom's legal structure: interpreting twelfth-century law', *Tijdschrift voor Rechtsgeschiedenis* 59 (1991), pp. 57–9; John Hudson, 'Anglo-Norman land law and the origins of property', in *Law and Government*, eds Garnett and Hudson, pp. 198–222.
27 M. Chibnall, *Anglo-Norman England, 1066–1166* (Oxford, 1986; repr. 1995), pp. 165–6.
28 J. C. Holt, 'Feudal society and the family in early medieval England', *TRHS*, 5th ser., 32–5 (1982–85): pt 1 (1982), pp. 193–212; pt 2 (1983), pp. 193–220; pt 3 (1984), pp. 1–25; pt 4 (1985), pp. 1–28.
29 Holt, 'Feudal society', pt 1: 'The revolution of 1066', p. 198.
30 *Ibid.*, p. 200.
31 See below, pp. 104–5.
32 Stenton, *First Century*, pp. 37–40.
33 Holt, 'Feudal society', pt 4: 'The heiress and the alien', pp. 2–10.
34 Judith Green, 'Aristocratic women in early twelfth-century England', *Anglo-*

Norman Political Culture and the Twelfth-Century Renaissance, ed. C. Warren Hollister (Woodbridge, Suffolk, 1997), pp. 59–82.

35 Maxine Berg, *A Woman in History. Eileen Power, 1889–1940* (Cambridge, 1996), pp. 66–72.

36 See *ibid.* for a list of Eileen Power's published works.

37 Doris Stenton, *The English Woman in History* (London, 1957).

38 Pollock and Maitland, *History of English Law*, 2, pp. 437–8.

39 D. Stenton, *English Woman*, p. 28.

40 Henry Loyn, *Anglo-Saxon England and the Norman Conquest* (London, 1962), pp. 323–4.

41 See above, pp. 102–3.

42 Marc A. Meyer, 'Early Anglo-Saxon penitentials and the position of women', *Haskins Society Journal* 2 (1990), pp. 47–61.

43 Marc A. Meyer, 'Women's estates in later Anglo-Saxon England: the politics of possession', *Haskins Society Journal* 3 (1991), pp. 111–30, at pp. 113–17.

44 Pauline Stafford, 'Women and the Norman Conquest', *TRHS*, 6th ser., 4 (1994), pp. 221–49.

45 *Ibid.*, pp. 227–8.

46 *Ibid.*, p. 240.

47 G. Duby, 'Women and power', in *Cultures of Power. Lordship, Status and Process in Twelfth-Century Europe*, ed. Thomas N. Bisson (Philadelphia, 1995), pp. 69–85.

48 Pauline Stafford, *Queen Emma and Queen Edith* (Oxford, 1983).

49 *Ibid.*, p. 107 and Appendix II.

50 *Ibid.*, p. 142.

51 *Ibid.*, pp. 82–94; Frank Barlow, *Edward the Confessor* (London, 1970), pp. 54–5.

52 See above, pp. 103–4.

53 Stafford, *Emma and Edith*, pp. 82–9.

54 The question of how far succession to England and Normandy was determined by existing family law and how far by royal custom is discussed by J. Le Patourel, 'The Norman succession, 996–1135', *English Historical Review* 86 (1971), pp. 225–50; E. Z. Tabuteau, 'The rule of law in the succession to Normandy and England, 1087', *Haskins Society Journal* 3 (1991), pp. 141–69; Barbara English, 'William the Conqueror and the Anglo-Norman succession', *Historical Research* 64 (1991), pp. 221–36; R. H. C. Davis, 'William of Jumièges, Robert Curthose and the Norman succession', *English Historical Review* 95 (1986), pp. 597–606; R. H. C. Davis, *From Alfred the Great to Stephen* (London and Rio Grande, 1991), pp. 131–40.

55 *The 'Gesta Guillelmi' of William of Poitiers*, eds R. H. C. Davis and M. Chibnall, OMT (Oxford, 1998), pp. xxvii, 150–3.

56 G. Garnett, 'Coronation and propaganda: some implications of the Norman claim to the throne of England in 1066', *TRHS* 36 (1986), pp. 91–116.

57 C. Warren Hollister, 'Normandy, France and the Anglo-Norman *regnum*', *Speculum* 51 (1976), pp. 202–42; his *Monarchy, Magnates and Institutions*, pp. 17–57; Davis, 'The Norman succession'.

58 Chibnall, *The Empress Matilda* (Oxford, 1997), pp. 205–6. The possibility of the right to the English crown being transmitted by a woman appears to have

been in the minds of the rebel barons in 1217, when they attempted to bring in Prince Louis (later Louis VIII of France) as king of England, on the grounds that John's rule had been illegitimate and that the right to the throne had passed to Louis through his wife Blanche of Castile, granddaughter of Henry II. *(The Letters and Charters of Cardinal Guala Bicchieri, papal legate in England 1216–1218*, ed. N. Vincent, Canterbury and York Society (Woodbridge, Suffolk, 1996), p. xl.

59 Stafford, *Emma and Edith*, pp. 86–7; M. K. Lawson, *Cnut: The Danes in England in the early eleventh century* (London, 1993), p. 115.

60 D. Bates, 'The origin of the justiciarship', *Anglo-Norman Studies* 4 (1982), pp. 1–12.

61 D. C. Douglas, 'The earliest Norman counts', *English Historical Review* 61 (1946), pp. 129–56.

62 Bates, 'Justiciarship'; F. West, *The Justiciarship in England, 1066–1232* (Cambridge 1966), pp. 2–30.

63 Bates, 'Justiciarship', p. 12; C. Warren Hollister, 'The rise of administrative kingship', in *Monarchy, Magnates and Institutions*, pp. 223–45.

64 Lois L. Huneycutt, 'The idea of the perfect princess: the *Life of St Margaret* in the reign of Matilda II (1100–1118)', *Anglo-Norman Studies* 12 (1990), pp. 81–97; Laura Wertheimer, 'Adeliza of Louvain and Anglo-Norman queenship', *Haskins Society Journal* 7 (1995), pp. 101–15.

65 Stafford, *Emma and Edith*, pp. 143–59; Chibnall, *Empress Matilda*, pp. 23–4, 28–9, 177–90.

8

The later twentieth century: empire and colonisation

The term 'empire' has been applied to various medieval political structures that brought together a number of distinct regional societies under a single ruler. The Roman empire, which persisted with its centre in Constantinople, and the Carolingian empire, which claimed to be a continuation of the Roman empire, preserved to some extent the classical meaning of the word. But imperial titles were sometimes attributed without classical connotations to Spanish kings, or to the tenth-century West Saxon kings.[1] James Ramsay chose 'The Angevin Empire' as a convenient title for a volume of medieval English history dealing with the Angevin rulers, but he used the title without deep meaning.[2] Serious concern with ideas of empire became much more widespread and critical in the 1960s.

In 1966 a meeting of the Société Jean Bodin considered the theme of 'Les grands empires'. On that occasion John Gilissen set out the characteristics that in his opinion ought to exist for the term 'empire' to be used.[3] There should be at least one great power in the regional structure, which should (within that structure) possess the requisite qualities of a sovereign state: concentration of power, complex composition, tendency to hegemony (at least regional), more extensive territory than that of other states, relatively long existence. In arguing that the Normans met the requirements of Gilissen, and deciding to call the book he was then writing the 'Norman empire', John Le Patourel used these criteria as a tool of analysis. He never said that they constituted a 'model'; and he was prepared to find variant details.[4] Norman domination in his account took the form of feudal lordship: 'rather an aristocratic domination than a mass settlement of Scandinavian peoples on Gallic soil'. The conquest of England 'became an overwhelming aristocratic and ecclesiastical colonization'. Colonisation spread to Scotland, and conquest and colonisation into Wales; overlordship was extended in northern France.

In this Le Patourel noted regional differences; and although the aristocratic domination was organised into a political structure, William's royal status was never extended to his rule in Normandy, even though his personal power there was kingly. The emphasis is on 'feudal overlordship'; Norman rule was not that of any modern sovereign state:

> The Norman king's rights over the king of Scots, the Welsh princes, the duke of Brittany and so on were clearly limited; but his rights over the barons, knights, religious institutions, and even the peasantry, within Normandy and England, were also limited to a greater or lesser extent by their various rights and liberties.[5]

Le Patourel never lost sight of the eleventh- and twelfth-century context in which he wrote of empire. At the same time, the monopolisation of a disproportionate amount of the wealth of the lands the Normans occupied was, to him, imperialism of at least one kind; and in their exploitation of the lands they conquered they showed some of the spirit of conquest that 'has so often lain at the root of imperialist ideas in other lands'. His purpose was never to attempt to impose twentieth-century notions of imperialism and colonialism on the Norman 'empire'. Moreover both in *The Norman Empire* and in his Stenton lecture he was asking questions rather than making dogmatic assertions,[6] and even his more positive answers were still tentative. He expressed the hope that he had initiated a debate, as indeed he had.

Le Patourel's work came at a time of changing historical interests, when a new approach to Anglo-Norman history was needed. A Channel-islander by birth and upbringing, he both put the subject into its European context and 'changed the accepted view of the Norman settlement derived from Round and Stenton'. As J. C. Holt wrote,

> His main intent ... was to emphasize the continental aspect of

English history, then to work the history of England and Normandy into a picture of a coherent Anglo-Norman world, neither wholly English nor wholly French, deserving study in its own right and on its own terms, terms which required that each part owed something to the other and to the whole …. More than any earlier historian he grasped the fact that the Norman Conquest had to be viewed as a process of colonization. Round's cataclysm, in which Norman rule was imposed almost cut and dried, was replaced by a much subtler picture of a more complex process in which frontiers were established progressively and the great baronies of Norman England were formed in stages.[7]

He had hoped to carry on his work by looking more deeply into the nature of Angevin rule; unhappily he died before he could make more than a beginning. This investigation is now in the hands of others.

The concept of empire involved the wider implications of the Norman Conquest. It was not simply a conquest of England; it included also colonisation in Scotland, and conquest and colonisation in Wales, and later in parts of Ireland. If one of the characteristics of 'empire' as Le Patourel had defined it was the concentration of power, the centre of power had to be indicated. And here a difficulty becomes apparent, for once William became king and took over the government and traditions of the English kingdom, Normandy was no longer the centre, however much time the king spent there, and however important the more-than-metropolitan status of Rouen may have become.[8] Le Patourel made much of the close links between England and Normandy, strengthened by the 'cross-channel' families and their desire to maintain a union of the two parts.[9] Warren Hollister, who built on Le Patourel's foundations, wrote of an Anglo-Norman *regnum*; a single realm united by a central authority, but not a sovereign state in the later medieval and modern sense.[10] An alternative appellation was a 'feudal empire', which emphasised lordship and personal bonds.

Like Le Patourel, Warren Hollister focused on the European setting of the *regnum*. His work, carried on for over thirty years in the medieval studies centre he built up in California at Santa Barbara, was particularly concerned with the reign of Henry I; he, and some of the pupils he trained and inspired, published a

steady stream of important articles on the period.[11] The comple-
tion of the biography of King Henry that he was writing was
delayed by misfortune; first the total destruction of his house and
most of his notes in a disastrous fire, and then, when only two or
three chapters remained to write, by his own sudden death. Two
of his pupils are working on the final chapters, and publication is
likely within two or three years.

Much fundamental work on Norman expansion into particular
regions has been done in the past quarter century. R. R. Davies has
shown how the Norman advance into Wales took the form of the
establishment of lordships, particularly by Hugh earl of Chester and
his cousin Robert of Rhuddlan in the north, and by William fitz
Osbern along the north shore of the Severn estuary in the south.[12]
But this penetration, made possible by the political fragmentation
of Wales at the time, varied greatly in the measure of control exercised; and when Davies first used the word 'colonisation' it was to
describe the earlier Saxon settlements in the areas of Wales where
Norman control was to be most easily established.[13] Of the
Normans his preferred terms were at first 'conquest' and 'settlement'; while 'colonising' is used, for example, in the establishment
of settlers from England (later from Flanders) in Welsh manors and
knights' fees.[14]

In a more detailed account of the nature of Anglo-Norman
settlement he showed that many of the greatest marcher lords had
interests elsewhere in England, Normandy and other parts of
France, and that much of the settlement was effected by their
vassals, so that 'the Norman conquest of Wales was rarely more
than the sum of individual baronial enterprises'.[15] Much effort
was needed to convert military commands into effective territorial lordships based on castles, which became a focus for
colonisation. At first even the vassals and their sub-tenants, who
extended their lordship over peasants, did not expropriate the
native settlers and replace them with English peasants.[16]
Colonisation brought the most fundamental changes initially in
the new boroughs, which were established around castles and
immediately attracted foreign settlers. In time a deeper colonisation took place; in the vale of Montgomery, for instance,
colonists were settled on waste lands; and elsewhere many small
free tenancies owing military services were established. The most

brutal form of colonisation was effected by the Flemings, who settled with Henry I's permission in Pembrokeshire; here settlement was organised under leaders of the 'locator' type, possibly retired mercenaries from the armies of Henry I, who established an identifiably Flemish colony in Dyfed.[17] Some groups moved on later into Ireland. This, however, was an exceptional type of alien colony; and Davies showed that the process of colonisation was patchy and difficult to chronicle.[18] Even if, by the end of the twelfth century, Wales was 'a country of two peoples, Welsh and Anglo-Norman', the Normans, here as elsewhere, were able to assimilate the traditions and institutions of the people whom they conquered. Cultural assimilation worked both ways. Davies did not attempt to impose a general definition of colonisation on the process of Norman and Anglo-Norman settlement in Wales.

There is no doubt that the process of settlement was very different in Scotland. In that realm no conquest took place; Anglo-Norman (or, it is sometimes said, Anglo-continental) settlers moved in by infiltration, often by invitation.[19] The movement has been most fully described by Geoffrey Barrow. The country was 'far from depopulated, but settled loosely and extensively enough for newcomers to enter by royal favour and practice a more intensive exploitation of resources'.[20] The marriage of Edgar Ætheling's sister Margaret to King Malcolm Canmore bound the royal families in close kinship. Some kind of dependence existed from the time that King Malcolm met King William at Abernethy in 1072 and, in the words of the *Anglo-Saxon Chronicle*, 'made peace with King William and gave hostages and was his man'.[21] Later, in 1079, he renewed his earlier promises and gave hostages to William's son, William Rufus.[22] This appears to have been a type of homage in the marches; the exact implications were open to different interpretations. Although the Norman kings of England could claim some form of lordship over Scotland, it had many of the ambiguities of the French kings' claims over Normandy.[23] Within the kingdom of the Scots, however, the immigrants entered by invitation, as kinsfolk, dependents or servants, and not as predators or conquerors. The new aristocratic settlers fitted in with the old, and were important in reinforcing the authority of the king of Scots. Many settlers came from 'the middle band of Anglo-continental settlers'; many came from families previously settled in Yorkshire, Cumbria or Northumberland.[24] Their integration in the kingdom of the Scots resulted in a blending of cultures, and greatly 'reinforced the Middle English elements in Scots speech and culture'.[25] The whole movement was part of the general expansion of colonisation beyond the moving frontiers. Scotland, as Barrow described it, was a land of opportunity for third sons.[26] The immigration into Scotland could usefully be compared with the kind of colonisation broadly treated in a European setting by Robert Bartlett, which often involved the extension of existing lordships or the creation of new ones rather than the permanent subjection of one political entity to another.[27]

In Ireland the Norman Conquest came later, beginning in the reign of Henry II. Robin Frame has shown that here colonisation was deeper. From 1169 Anglo-Norman settlers took advantage of conflicts between the Irish rulers to enter by invitation and settle with the military backing of Henry II.[28] They also brought English, Welsh and Flemish peasants to work the soil in the lordships they established, and there were later implants of migrants from Scotland in Ulster.[29] Frame argued, however, that to see a colonial pattern in this involved taking a long view.[30] David Walker took up the point and gave a salutary warning that it is not easy to assess the scale of a building-up of hostility to the alien settlers of the twelfth and early thirteenth centuries:

> There is a danger that we may see the racial tensions of this period in terms more appropriate to a later century. The increasing pressure of lordship in the later middle ages, the invasion of the north, sponsored by Robert Bruce and carried out by Edward Bruce in 1315, the resurgence of English interest in the reign of Richard II – all made for increasing friction. Still later the potent mixture of dynastic and religious policies under the Tudors and Stuarts exacerbated older tensions .... All that can introduce emotional overtures and distortions into our interpretation of Anglo-Norman Ireland.[31]

This warning is a reminder that, however, stimulating analogies between movements such as territorial expansion and colonisation in different centuries may be, it is perilous to try to leap across the centuries. Peoples involved in colonising other lands in the twelfth no less than in the twentieth century sometimes justified their actions by claiming that they brought a higher civilisation to barbarous peoples, but there was not an inevitable, or even a probable, clear line of development through eight centuries.

One outcome of the debate has been to suggest that a new approach to the political structure of Europe in the later age of Norman expansion is necessary. Interest has grown in the loose grouping of political and economic societies in northern France and other parts of Europe, and the particular stresses of the frontier regions. David Bates, for example, while accepting the value of Le Patourel's basic thesis that 'the cross-Channel aristocracy created after 1066 had a strong vested interest in maintaining the union of Normandy and England', insisted on the importance of the Norman families whose main interests were on one side of the Channel, and on the cross-frontier aristocracy with lands in both Normandy and France.[32] He also urged a need for a further 'discussion of economic and cultural relations, as well as a positive acceptance of the potentialities of modern theories of colonialism'.[33]

These theories need to be handled with caution. It is difficult, if not impossible, to apply later patterns of empire-building at all closely to the Norman hegemony. Even more inappropriate in such a setting are the words 'imperialism' and 'colonialism' with their pejorative associations. As long ago as 1950 Keith Hancock wrote that 'imperialism' was no word for scholars: it was a pseudo-concept which set out to make everything clear and ended by making everything muddled.[34] Forty years after Hancock, when Brian Golding discussed the characteristics of Normandy, he cited the comment of B. Bartel that 'there are so many definitions of colonialism and imperialism as to make the terms almost useless'.[35] The discussion has been further confused by the inappropriate use of the term 'model', as when David Bates criticised Le Patourel for using a 'model of colonisation' that was 'excessively simplified and one-dimensional', although Le Patourel avoided ever using the term 'model'.[36]

Francis West, in an article published in *History*, has provided an outline of the confusions which have arisen from colonial and imperial approaches to the Norman Conquest.[37] Modern colonial history can sometimes suggest useful lines of enquiry, occasionally even interesting analogies. Some modern assumptions would be inappropriate: no one looks in the twelfth century for the 'executive-led government of colonial rule' of the twentieth.[38] But any historian who draws comparisons needs to start by carefully defining what he means by 'empire' or 'colony', and hoping that he will not then be attacked for not adopting a different and possibly unhistorical approach to a difficult and currently very emotive subject. Such abstracts as 'colonialism' and 'imperialism', Francis West argued, are of no use to Anglo-Norman historians, though there are some things in the theory and practice of modern colonial administration that can suggest useful lines of enquiry. He suggested approaches through the character of land tenure, which has economic, religious and social values in varying proportions, or the question of legitimacy deriving from indirect rule.

J. C. Holt, who took up the legacy of Le Patourel constructively and with historical imagination, has looked at 'colonial England' in the topics of buildings, language and law.[39] Robert Bartlett examined the ways in which common elements in culture distinguished different imperial settlements, suggesting that 'except where ethnic or religious difference existed between incoming and native populations, colonial aristocracies became, eventually, no different from non-colonial aristocracies'.[40] Brian Golding, sceptical of the use of inappropriate general concepts, sifted out some general observations. He pointed to

> one fundamental difference between the Norman colonisation of England and many, though not all, imperial settlements. England and Normandy largely shared a common culture. Above all, they were both members of the western Church under the papacy, which was itself at the time establishing itself as a spiritual empire with an overarching hegemony.[41]

This brings out the importance of two general movements taking place over western Europe: the economic expansion with all that it implied in terms of the commercialisation of society, and the religious reforms that brought fundamental changes into the structure and social ideals of the Western Church.[42] The colonial angle is one (but only one) of the ways in which the Norman Conquest in its wider setting might profitably be investigated.

Notes

1 R. Folz, *L'Idée d'Empire en Occident* (Paris, 1953), pp. 49–54; J. Le Patourel, *The Norman Empire* (Oxford, 1976), pp. 58–9, 323 n. 1. See also N. Higham, *An English Empire* (Manchester, 1995).

2 J. H. Ramsay, *The Angevin Empire, 1154–1216* (London, 1903), vol. 3 of *The Scholar's History of England*.

3 John Gilissen, 'La notion d'empire dans l'histoire universelle', *Recueil de la Société Jean Bodin*, 31 (1966), pp. 281–3.

4 Le Patourel, *Norman Empire*, p. v.

5 *Ibid.*, p. 321.

6 *Ibid.*, ch. 9, esp. pp. 323–5; J. Le Patourel, *Feudal Empires, Norman and Plantagenet* (London, 1984), no. 7; 'Normandy and England, 1066–1144' (Stenton Lecture).

7. J. C. Holt,' John Le Patourel', *Proceedings of the British Academy* 71 (1985), pp. 583–96, at pp. 593–4.

8 C. H. Haskins, *Norman Institutions* (Cambridge, Massachusetts, 1925), p. 144.

9 Le Patourel, 'Normandy and England', pp. 7–9.

10 C. Warren Hollister, 'Normandy, France and the Anglo-Norman *regnum*', in his *Monarchy, Magnates and Institutions in the Anglo-Norman World* (London and Ronceverte, 1986), pp. 17–57.

11 Some of Hollister's most important papers have been published in *Monarchy, Magnates and Institutions*.

12 R. R. Davies, *Conquest, Coexistence, and Change: Wales, 1063–1415* (Oxford, 1987), ch. 2.

13 Davies, *Conquest, Coexistence*, p. 26.

14 *Ibid.*, p. 37.

15 *Ibid.*, p. 87. One aspect of the settlement, the movement of settlers from one area to another, which Davies calls 'internal expansion' rather than 'colonisation', is described by David Walker, *The Normans in Britain* (Oxford, England, and Cambridge, Massachusetts), pp. 60–61.

16 Davies, *Conquest, Coexistence*, p. 96.

17 I. A. Rowlands, 'Aspects of the Norman settlement in Dyfed', *Anglo-Norman Studies* 3 (1981), pp. 142–57; M. Chibnall. '"Racial" minorities in the Anglo-Norman realm', in *Minorities and Barbarians in Medieval Life*, eds S. J. Ridyard and R. G. Benson (Sewanee, Tennessee, 1996), pp. 49–61.

18 Davies, *Conquest, Coexistence*, pp. 99–100.

19 G. W. S. Barrow, *The Anglo-Norman Era in Scottish History* (Oxford, 1980), pp. 92–3.

20 Barrow, *Anglo-Norman Era*, p. 50. See also Walker, *Normans in Britain*, p. 92.

21 *Anglo-Saxon Chronicle*, s.a.1072 (*E*), 1073 (*D*).

22 Frank Barlow, *William Rufus* (London, 1983), pp. 288–95.

23 Hollister, 'Normandy, France and the Anglo-Norman *regnum*', pp. 17–57.

24 Barrow, *Anglo-Norman Era*, pp. 105–17.

25 *Ibid.*, p. 117.

26 *Ibid.*, pp. 12–29.

27 Robert Bartlett, 'Colonial aristocracies of the High Middle Ages', in *Medieval*

Frontier Societies, eds R. Bartlett and A. Mackay (Oxford, 1989), pp. 23–47, at p. 24.

28 Robin Frame, *Colonial Ireland* (Dublin, 1981), pp. 7–19.

29 Walker, *Normans in Britain*, p. 22; Frame, *Colonial Ireland*, pp. viii, 26, 69–70.

30 Robin Frame, *English Lordship in Ireland, 1318–1361* (Oxford, 1982).

31 Walker, *Normans in Britain*, p. 115.

32 David Bates,'Normandy and England after 1066', *English Historical Review* 104 (1989), pp. 851–80, at p. 859.

33 *Ibid.*, p. 861.

34 W. K. Hancock, *The Wealth of Colonies* (Cambridge, 1950), p. 8.

35 B. Bartel, 'Comparative historical archaeology and archaeological theory', in *Comparative Studies in the Archaeology of Colonisation*, ed. S. L. Dyson (Oxford, 1985), p. 9.

36 Bates, 'Normandy and England', p. 863.

37 F. J. West, 'The colonial history of the Norman conquest', *History*, 84 (1999), pp. 219–36. I am grateful to Professor West for lending me a copy of this article before publication.

38 Leading article on Hong Kong in the *Financial Times*, 30 June 1998.

39 J. C. Holt, *Colonial England, 1066–1232* (London and Rio Grande, 1997), pp. 1–24; Le Patourel also wrote of buildings as a sign of dominion (*Norman Empire*, pp. 351–3).

40 Robert Bartlett, *The Making of Europe: Conquest, Colonization and Cultural Change, 950–1350* (London, 1993), p. 59.

41 Brian Golding, *Conquest and Colonisation: The Normans in Britain, 1066–1100* (Oxford, 1994), p. 179.

42 See below, ch. 10.

9

The later twentieth century:
peoples and frontiers

In 1993 R. R. Davies opened the first of his presidential addresses to the Royal Historical Society on 'The peoples of Great Britain and Ireland, 1100–1400' with the statement, 'Peoples are back on the historian's agenda'. He attributed this partly to 'the growing awareness of the power of ethnicity in our contemporary world' and partly to

> the growing recognition that the centrality that historians have so long given to the unitary nation–state as the natural, inevitable and indeed desirable unit of human power and political organisation is itself a reflection of the intellectual climate in which modern academic historiography was forged in the nineteenth century.[1]

This caught the mood of the change that had gradually been taking place in historical studies. It was a change that explains the reaction against Le Patourel's view of a Norman empire which, new as it was when he expressed it, had ceased to answer the kind of questions being asked by historians whose central interests had shifted rather more to 'peoples' and 'nations' in the medieval sense, and to looser, more transient 'empires' that could be described in very modern terms as 'federations' of peoples. Although Gaimar, describing the reign of Edgar who 'held the land as emperor, and ruled over the Scots and the Welsh' added that 'Never since Arthur had any king such power' he did not actually use the word 'federation', which Davies introduced into his translation.[2]

A broad general definition of a nation was provided in 1941 by V. H. Galbraith, who wrote, 'A nation may be defined as any considerable group of people who believe they *are* one' and added of the sentiment of nationality:

> Its minimum content is love, or at least awareness, of one's country, and pride in its past achievements, real or fictitious; and it springs from attachment to the known and familiar stimulated by the perception of difference – difference of habits and customs, often too of speech, from those of neighbouring peoples.[3]

He added, however, that personal lordship 'cut across and in some ways blunted the edge of nationalism' in the Middle Ages, and was an important force making for social coherence; indeed, that nationalism was then 'relatively inconspicuous'. Putting this another way, the idea of the Norman people (*gens Normannorum*) was a potent force in the time of great Norman expansion, whereas much less is heard of any Norman nation (*nacio*). The inspiration for this idea came from the Norman origin-myth.

The Norman myth was brought into the centre of historical debate by R. H. C. Davis in his book on *The Normans and their Myth*.[4] He looked behind the Norman expansion, described in its greatest detail by C. H. Haskins and D. C. Douglas,[5] to investigate the myth that sustained it. Origin myths were an essential part of the self-awareness of the various peoples who had settled within the crumbling fabric of the Roman empire, and had established kingdoms or principalities of their own.[6] All emphasised descent from some pagan god, or later, with the acceptance of Christianity, from some ancient hero. The peoples taking over the Roman heritage were inspired by the Roman legend, popularised by Vergil, of the foundation of Rome by Aeneas after his escape from burning Troy. They looked for Trojan ancestors. After the viking northmen had settled in the lower Seine basin under their count of Rouen, and had gradually built up a new principality, its status as a duchy under a leader styling himself 'count' (later 'duke') of Normandy was given official recognition by the Capetian kings. Its earlier history was given an official stamp in the early eleventh century by the historian, Dudo of Saint Quentin.[7] He gave literary shape to the origin-myth, and read back conditions prevailing at the time he wrote into the first days of the settlement a century before. In his version of the story, the first settlers under their leader Rollo came from 'Dacia', and were descended indirectly from a group of Trojans led by a certain Antenor. Rollo had become baptised and had married a daughter of Charles the Simple, so legitimising his rule.[8] From the beginning, however, the Norman myth was different from other origin-myths. Dudo described a strange vision that had come to Rollo before he began the conquest of Normandy, in which he found himself on the top of a high mountain in Francia, and bathed in a wonderful spring which cured him of leprosy. Then birds of many kinds came in turn to bathe in the same spring, before building their nests and living together in amity at his command.[9] The vision was interpreted to mean that after his baptism Rollo would rule over many peoples who had come together from many nations to become a single people.

This acceptance of the very mixed racial population of Danish and Norwegian vikings, Franks, Bretons and Flemings which made up the Norman people from the first was exceptional in origin-myths. Although Rollo was claimed as a descendant of the Trojan Antenor, he ruled over a mixed people, and its strength was in the mixture.[10] As an eleventh-century monk of Saint-Wandrille wrote shortly before the conquest of England, Rollo quickly reconciled 'the men of all origins and different occupations, and made a single people out of the various peoples'.[11] This was the central theme in the Norman myth, to be repeated with variations by a line of Norman historians who lived and worked in Normandy, from William of Jumièges to Orderic Vitalis.[12] With minor adaptations it was appropriate for the great period of Norman expansion which was coming to an end when Orderic wrote. Orderic gave the myth the shape which, after the revival of interest in his work in the nineteenth century, was to receive a new lease of life.[13] The contrast between his view of the Norman people and that of his younger contemporary, Henry archdeacon of Huntingdon, makes clear that it was ceasing to be appropriate for the descendants of Norman conquerors living in England, even when they were of mixed blood.[14] The myth has provided a useful angle of approach to the Norman Conquest.

The racial mix in Duke William's army in 1066 is reflected in Graeme Ritchie's light-hearted reference to 'Duke William's Breton, Lotharingian, Flemish, Picard, Artesian, Cenomanian,

Angevin, general-French and Norman Conquest'.[15] Their leader, however, was recognised as the 'duke of the Normans', and his fellow-countrymen thought of themselves as a single Norman people. William of Poitiers, writing his contemporary biography of the duke, was aware of different elements in the army: the distinction that he drew was that between the Breton and other auxiliaries who had joined the enterprise under their own leaders, and the men (whatever their origin, including some Bretons) who were directly under the duke and specially bound by oaths of fealty.[16] A subtle change of emphasis appears in his writing after the duke of Normandy had become king of England and had imposed a code of discipline on the soldiers in his army. Then, he alleged, the Normans were not given greater licence than the Bretons or Aquitanians; and Normans and Bretons all obeyed William as a most acceptable lord.[17] What, in modern politically correct language would be described as 'the Other', were the conquered people, the English.

For a time conquerors and conquered were distinguished as Normans (or *Franci*) and English; but there was some doubt about who, in the racially very mixed conquered kingdom, ought to be described as English. Before Henry of Huntingdon died it was quite plain that, to many, the English people included some Normans. No wonder Huntingdon was somewhat inconsistent in his terminology, and modern historians have often been confused. As Ralph Davis put it, 'the paradox of the Normans is that though it was in England that they reached their acme and fulfilled themselves as Normans, yet in the long run the conquest of England turned them into Englishmen'.[18] The date when the Normans in England can be said to have disappeared came, in his view, certainly before the end of the twelfth century, so that the loss of Normandy in 1204 merely 'put the seal on a development which was already virtually complete'. In one place Davis suggested that in some ways the English were becoming Norman by about 1140;[19] this has been endorsed with greater subtlety by more recent historians. In particular, John Gillingham, who has devoted a number of articles to the question, suggests a date somewhere in the late 1130s.[20] This is borne out both by the various revisions that Henry of Huntingdon made in his 'History of the English', and by the vernacular *Estoire des Engleis* written by Geoffrey Gaimar for his patroness, the wife of Ralph fitz Gilbert.[21]

Henry of Huntingdon in places used the term 'English' to include all the peoples living in England before 1066, including a sprinkling of Normans who had come in the wake of Edward the Confessor. In describing the immediate impact of the conquest he wrote that 'scarcely a noble of English descent remained in England, but all were reduced to servitude and distress, so that it was shameful even to be called English'.[22] In this context the English were identified as the conquered, who were ruled by the Normans. Yet in the continuation and revision of his history, written in the early 1140s, he clearly thought of himself as one of the English, and called them 'our people'.[23] Orderic Vitalis had been born in England in 1075 and called himself *'angligena'* (of English race); but after spending the greater part of his life in Normandy, in daily contact with Normans who had kept their Norman roots, he did not think of the English in this way.[24] John Gillingham has suggested that at times Henry of Huntingdon's differentiation between English and Normans may even correspond to divisions in the aristocracy at King Stephen's court.[25] This in turn might depend on whether the bulk of their estates and interests lay in England or Normandy.

Though this might have seemed a passing phase resulting from civil war, there was a reality behind it. Some branches of Norman families who had made their homes in England were becoming so acclimatised that they spent most of their lives there, when not following the king's court if it visited Normandy; they arranged marriages to consolidate their English estates, endowed English monasteries and chose to be buried in them, rather than continuing their former patronage of abbeys in Normandy.[26] Other branches remained rooted in their Norman patrimonies, possibly using any minor English estates they had acquired to enlarge the endowments of the alien priories their ancestors had established across the Channel in England. Before the end of the twelfth century they were carefully calling themselves Normans as distinct from French, and cherishing the 'custom of Normandy'. As Philippe Contamine wrote, 'the Normans formed one of the nations and peoples whose identity appears extremely vigorous in the context of the rather nebulous French identity of the period'.[27] The sense of belonging to a particular people is one further element to set beside law and administration to suggest that the most lasting consequences of the Norman Conquest became visible only some eighty or a hundred years after 1066. Stephen's troubled reign may have given a jolt to some of the changes, but it was a relatively minor interruption.

So what, we may reasonably ask, were the essential elements in defining a people? In the polyglot kingdom of England the position was complicated linguistically by the existence of Latin and French as the languages of government, with French as the speech of the aristocracy and the *lingua franca* of Western Europe.[28] Old English dropped out of use for official records soon after 1070, and when English reappeared slowly and tentatively from the mid-thirteenth century it was the language spoken by the people, the 'Middle English' which was far from uniform, and which Ranulf Higden described as having three main branches.[29] The multiplicity of dialects may have contributed to the persistence and even growing use of French in administration during the thirteenth and early fourteenth centuries, just as English continued in general use in India long after the ending of imperial rule. French was certainly important as a literary language, and as a language used in both secular and ecclesiastical courts long before it became a language of record. Dominica Legge liked to remember the comment of her teacher, Mildred Pope, 'I'm beginning to think that Anglo-Norman was only written French', and it is true that a wealth of French literature was produced in England during the twelfth century.[30] However, slight differences in the written language were appearing by the time Philippe de Thaon wrote his *Comput* in the second decade of the twelfth century, so that French and Anglo-Norman gradually moved apart.[31]

At the same time French, as the language of administration, was essential for the upwardly mobile. When Wulfric of Haselbury loosed the tongue of a dumb man who immediately began to speak fluently in English and French, his loyal servant, the priest Brictric, took offence, saying, 'I've served you for years, all for nothing. You've never enabled me to speak French, and when I come before the bishop and the archdeacon I have to stand as dumb as any mute'.[32] In the local shire and hundred courts the languages spoken must have been both English and French, even though the record was kept in Latin. And there is still speculation about the language spoken in the home. Ian Short has suggested that 'English ... needs to be viewed as the class-inclusive vernacular not only of the native population, but also of the French-speaking minority. These must have acquired it ... as a natural second language from as early as the second or third post-Conquest generations'.[33] Ian Short saw trilingualism as common, and came to the conclusion that by the mid-twelfth century most of the 'Anglo-Normans' would probably have had a command of English for practical purposes, and that it would almost certainly have been their first language by the end of the century.[34] Michael Clanchy, on the other hand, has questioned their trilingualism; and has argued that it was not primarily the Norman Conquest, but the advance of French as an international literary and cultural language, particularly in the thirteenth century, which caused its increasing use as a written language for English needs.[35] On the subject of language different interpretations are not surprising, since the evidence, particularly of the language spoken in the home, is very slight, and the known examples may not be typical.

Fourteenth-century writers could not avoid being struck by the diversity of languages within England, and some commented on it. To Higden the Norman Conquest was the first cause of the debasement of the English language, and the original use of French. Like most of his contemporaries, however, he did not treat this explicitly as a grievance; and within a generation his translator, John Trevisa, had noted the rapid decline of French in the homes even of the gentry. What the chroniclers brought out clearly, however, was the influence of the conquest on the language of their country.[36] Even when their comments were simply observations, later writers could easily seize on them as an indication of the French-speaking Normans as oppressors. D. Moffat has even found in them 'an expression of racial disharmony as another factor that contributed significantly to the dynamics of medieval society'.[37] This is very questionable, as it seems to be reading back modern racial tensions into the later Middle Ages.

Law was another important element included in medieval definitions of a people. Regino of Prüm wrote (c.900) that 'the various nations differ in descent, customs, language and law'.[38] Language was held to 'make a people' (*gentem lingua facit*).[39] When the Normans came to England the principle of 'personality of the law', characteristic of early medieval Europe, still persisted. William of Poitiers wrote of the 'laws of peoples', referring to the different customs of English and Normans.[40] Orderic Vitalis claimed that, in 1075, Earl Waltheof was executed for treason because he was English and was judged by English law; the other conspirators were punished by 'the laws of the Normans'.[41] The survival of local courts and legal procedures ensured that change would be slow, and that it would be particularly slow wherever there were strong regional customs.[42] Even at the aristocratic level, the emergence of a genuinely common law was gradual, and seems to have become evident about the time that the Normans felt themselves to be English. Variations remained in the frontier regions, and in the territories of Wales, Scotland and Ireland, to which the conquest spread more slowly and in different guises. Whereas Welsh law was still administered in some marcher lordships as late as the fourteenth century, serious attempts were being made to force all pleading into common-law forms in the parts of Ireland under English rule before the end of the twelfth century.[43]

Frontiers no less than peoples could be said to be firmly on the historian's agenda. The whole topic of the frontier was given a boost in 1893 by F. J. Turner's address to the American Historical Association on 'The significance of the frontier in American history'.[44] Turner saw the frontier as 'a form of society rather than an area. It is the term applied to a region whose social conditions result from the application of older institutions and ideas to the transforming influence of free land'. His interest was stimulated by the changes resulting from the closing of the frontier as settlement in America spread across the whole of the continent. It had for a time a considerable importance in American historical studies, but in the course of the past century has been largely rejected in the United States. As Robert I. Burns complained, 'When Turner's thinking did become clear, it was not very useful; when useful, it was not very clear'. However Burns himself, like many others among his contemporaries, 'remained affected by selected elements and particularly by its emphasis on social history'.[45]

Turner can have been at best no more than a contributory

influence on the work of medieval historians directly concerned with the fluctuating frontiers of the Anglo-Norman realm. Naturally there was a basic difference between conditions in the areas of Norman expansion bordering on Wales, Scotland, and Ireland, where the Norman settlers came into contact with people whose social customs and traditions differed greatly from their own, and the marches of Normandy itself, where the neighbouring principalities belonged essentially to the same culture. When Robert Bartlett contrasted a central, core area of the Frankish and German heartlands, together with England after 1066, with the Celtic and Slav peripheries, he was not concerned with internal frontiers such as these.[46] His rather arbitrary inclusion of England in the core area only after 1066 has already been challenged. Matthew Strickland asked how far Bartlett's division 'could hold true of the English kingdom which, by the early eleventh century had achieved a degree of political unification, governmental sophistication and economic development that rivalled, if not far outmatched, any of the political units existing within the "central area" of Europe?'.[47] This is a valid point, for 1066 is not a very satisfactory bench-mark in books dealing with general European development, any more than in studies confined to England or Normandy. There can, however, be general agreement on a difference between the character of the internal frontiers of the kingdom of France, and the frontiers separating kingdoms or principalities which differed in race, language and custom.

The Norman Conquest affected the frontiers of the English kingdom when it became the Norman base for further conquests into Wales, Scotland and Ireland.[48] In a different way, it affected the frontiers of the Norman duchy itself. Although these have often been treated as firm and stable from the mid-eleventh century, this may be due, as Daniel Power has suggested, to approaching the subject through an interest in ducal government, whereas 'the history of the aristocracy shows more movement'.[49] The distribution of the wealth of England to the Conqueror's companions created cross-Channel interests for many of the greatest Norman families, some of whom, as well as some who had no significant properties in England, had cross-border interests in the Vexin, the Passais and the region of Perche. There were struggles to control the border castles extending from

Ambrières and Gorron, through Moulins-la-Marche and Bellême, to Neufchatel and Gisors in the Vexin. Great families, such as the Bellême and the Beaumont counts of Meulan, had extensive lands in Normandy and France as well as in England, and their vassals too were spread across the borders. Marriage and inheritance could change the balance of interest in different regions; these and the fortunes of war influenced the aspirations of the leading magnates in the Anglo-Norman realm up to and even beyond the loss of Normandy in 1204. The conquest of England meant that the king/duke's relations with the king of France involved far more than his possible vassal status; they were bound up with the shaping of the French kingdom.

The cross-Channel estates may well have influenced the magnates in 1087 and 1135, when the possibility of Normandy and England ceasing to be under the same ruler had to be considered, and many lords opted to keep the realm united.[50] But a few generations of settlement changed the balance. Where patrimony and acquisitions descended in two different lines, the settlers in England sometimes put down roots within two generations. The experience of Stephen's reign, after Geoffrey of Anjou completed the conquest of Normandy in 1144, was a severe jolt to families that had tried to maintain a serious cross-Channel interest. Branches of families like the Tosny, once established on their English estates, began to become more identified with their new homeland, even though valuing their former Norman patrimonies.[51] Their patronage began to be directed to English monastic foundations rather than to the family monasteries in Normandy, and these new foundations became their chosen burial places.[52] Estates in England might be consolidated by marriage. Some great families like the Bellême and the Beaumonts tried to preserve major cross-Channel interests. Choice was taken from the Bellême, as Henri I confiscated all their English lands after the rebellion of Robert of Bellême in 1102; and Robert's descendants had to transfer their activities to their lands along the southern frontiers of Normandy.[53] For the Beaumonts, counts of Meulan, the wars of Stephen's reign were decisive; the twin brothers, Robert and Waleran shared the inheritance, with Robert taking the bulk of the English estates and Waleran those of the Beaumont patrimony in France and Normandy, where he suffered a setback through the Angevin advances in Normandy.[54]

Some less prominent families were compelled, by their experiences between 1137 and 1154, to realise that they might have to decide whether their real interests lay on the English or the French side of the Channel.[55] Stephen's reign gave a foretaste of the choice that had finally to be made in 1204. In his study of the frontier of Angevin Normandy, Daniel Power noted that 'families whose chief possessions lay within Normandy ceased to marry into families from *Francia*; ... the counts of Meulan used French dowries for their French marriages and Norman dowries for their Plantagenet matches'. Between about 1168 and 1181 the counts of Évreux, another frontier family, were 'transformed from being Franco-Norman magnates with no English lands into being Anglo-Norman lords with no French lands'.[56] Frontier studies are now providing new perspectives on the repercussions of the Norman Conquest on the French no less than on the English side of the Channel. The conclusions of different writers on the place of cross-Channel or cross-frontier estates is likely to depend on the timescale under consideration – a monograph concerned with changes up to 1135 or 1154 is likely to come to different conclusions from one extended to 1204 or 1215.

There is no doubt that the conquest of England by the Normans had important consequences for the Normans themselves in their homeland, though the extent of any changes has been a controversial subject. The status of the duke of Normandy as a crowned monarch reacted on his relations with the king of France. As J.-F. Lemarignier showed, during the eleventh century, if homage was ever performed it was 'homage in the marches', not in Paris; and it had some of the elements of a treaty of peace between two almost equal lords.[57] C. Warren Hollister has brought out the ambiguities both of the relationship and of William's status in Normandy: 'although William was never formally *rex Normannorum* he was an anointed king who governed the Normans in Normandy and England alike'.[58] Even if he had done homage in the marches to the boy-king Philip in 1060, that was before he had won a kingdom. Up to 1106 'at the time that Henry conquered Normandy from his brother, no crowned king of England had ever done homage to a king of France. Both Henry I and Stephen allowed their sons to do homage; Henry II was the first crowned king to do homage in person; moreover, he did it in Paris, not merely in the marches.[59]

For nearly a century the situation was ambiguous, with the English king preserving his status in Normandy, even though he might call himself merely 'protector of the Normans' on his seal.

The more controversial question which was asked by Le Patourel is whether there was assimilation in administration, law and custom, and art and literature, between England and Normandy. His conclusions were tentative:

> The question whether, in the most general sense, the lands and lord-
> ships of the Norman kings were moving towards an even closer
> integration in the last years of Henry Beauclerc, or whether there
> were already factors which would bring their integration to a halt at
> some point or even put the process into reverse, still cannot be
> answered with any assurance.[60]

He inclined, however, slightly to the side of greater assimilation. The opposite view has been taken up by a number of later historians, notably David Bates. He minimises the impact of English administrative practices in Normandy, and argues for a much greater strength in the forces making for eventually separate kingdoms of England and France than for a stable Normanno-English kingdom bestriding the Channel.[61] There is more general agreement that, in art and architecture and culture at least, a good deal of assimilation took place in the early twelfth century.[62]

Notes

1 R. R. Davies, 'The peoples of Great Britain and Ireland, 1100–1400: 1. Identities', *TRHS*, 6th ser., 4 (1994), pp. 1–20, at p. 1.

2 Geffrei Gaimar, *L'Estoire des Engleis,* Anglo-Norman Text Society, nos 14–16 (Oxford, 1960), lines 3561–8, p. 113.

3 V. H. Galbraith, 'Nationality and language in medieval England', *TRHS,* 4th ser., 23 (1941), pp. 113–28, at p. 113.

4 R. H. C. Davis, *The Normans and their Myth* (London, 1976).

5 See above, pp. 70–3.

6 S. Reynolds, 'Medieval *origines gentium* and the Community of the Realm', *History* 68 (1983), pp. 375–90.

7 Davis, *Normans and their Myth*, pp. 50–2; Dudo of St Quentin, *History of the Normans*, trans. Eric Christiansen (Woodbridge, Suffolk, 1998).

8 Dudo, *History*, Books 1 and 2.

9 *Ibid.*, pp. 29–30.

10 Cassandra Potts, '*Atque unum ex diversis gentibus populum effecit:* Historical tradition and the Norman identity', *Anglo-Norman Studies*, 18 (1996), pp. 139–52; Cassandra Potts, *Monastic Revival and Regional Identity in Early*

Normandy (Woodbridge, Suffolk, 1997), pp. 2–4.

11 *Inventio et miracula Sancti Vulfranni*, ed. Jean Laporte (Rouen, 1938); redated by E. M. C. van Houts, 'Historiography and hagiography at Saint-Wandrille', *Anglo-Norman Studies* 12 (1990), pp. 233–51.

12 The *'Gesta Normannorum Ducum'* of William of Jumièges, ed. E. M. C. van Houts, 2 vols, OMT (Oxford, 1992–5); *The Ecclesiastical History of Orderic Vitalis*, ed. M. Chibnall, OMT (Oxford, 1969–80).

13 *Orderic Vitalis*, 4, p. xiii.

14 See above, pp. 14–15.

15 R. L. Graeme Ritchie, *The Normans in Scotland* (Edinburgh, 1954), p. 157.

16 The *'Gesta Guillelmi'* of William of Poitiers, eds R. H. C. Davis and M. Chibnall, OMT (Oxford, 1988), pp. 128–9, 130–1.

17 *William of Poitiers*, pp. 160–1.

18. Davis, *Normans and their Myth*, p. 122.

19 *Ibid.*, pp. 132.

20 Reprinted, J. Gillingham, *The English in the Twelfth Century* (Woodbridge, 1999).

21 For Henry of Huntingdon, see above, pp. 14–15; Gaimar's *Estoire* has been dated by the editor (pp. li–lii) as 1135–40.

22 *Henry, archdeacon of Huntingdon, 'Historia Anglorum'*, ed. Diana Greenway, OMT (Oxford, 1996), pp. 402–3.

23 *Henry of Huntingdon*, pp. 715–19. See also John Gillingham, 'Henry of Huntingdon and the twelfth-century revival of the English nation', in *Concepts of National Identity in the Middle Ages*, eds S. Forde, L. Johnson and A. V. Murray, Leeds Texts and Monographs n.s. 14 (Leeds, 1995), pp. 75–101.

24 *Orderic Vitalis*, 5, pp. 6–7.

25 Gillingham, 'Henry of Huntingdon', p. 89.

26 L. Musset, 'Aux origines d'une classe dirigeante: les Tosny', *Francia* 5 (1978), pp. 45–80; B. Golding, 'Anglo-Norman knightly burials', *The Ideals and Practice of Medieval Knighthood* 1, eds C. Harper-Bill and R. Harvey (Woodbridge, Suffolk, 1986), pp. 35–48.

27 Gillingham, 'Henry of Huntingdon', p. 89; Philippe Contamine, 'The Norman 'nation' and the French 'nation', in the fourteenth and fifteenth centuries', *England and Normandy in the Middle Ages*, eds D. Bates and A. Curry (London and Rio Grande, 1994), pp. 215–34.

28 See above, pp. 20–1, 91.

29 See above, pp. 20–1.

30 Ian Short, 'Patrons and polyglots: French literature in twelfth-century England', *Anglo-Norman Studies* 14 (1992), pp. 229–50; M. D. Legge, 'Les origines de l'anglo-normand littéraire', *Revue de linguistique romane* 31 (1967), pp. 44–54; M. D. Legge, 'Anglo-Norman as a spoken language', *Anglo-Norman Studies* 2 (1980), p. 109.

31 *Philippe de Thaon, Comput*, ed. Ian Short, Anglo-Norman Text Society (London, 1984), vol. 2, lines 101–2; Ian Short, *'Tam Angli quam Franci: Self-definition in Anglo-Norman England'*, *Anglo-Norman Studies* 18 (1996), pp. 153–75, at p. 155 and n.6. I am grateful to Ian Short for these references.

32 *Wulfric of Haselbury by John, Abbot of Ford* (Somerset Record Society 47, 1933), p. 29; trans. P. Matarasso, in *A Gathering of Friends, The Learning*

and Spirituality of John of Forde, eds H. Costello and C. Holdsworth (Kalamazoo, Michigan, 1996), pp. 43–63, at p. 54.

33 Short, *'Tam Angli quam Franci',* p. 156.

34 Short, 'Patrons and polyglots', pp. 245–7.

35 M. T. Clanchy, *From Memory to Written Record: England, 1066–1307,* 2nd edn (Oxford, 1993), pp. 214–20.

36 See above, pp. 20–1.

37 D. Moffat, 'Sin, conquest, servitude: English self-image in the chronicles of the early fourteenth century', in *The Work of Work,* eds A. J. Frantzen and D. Moffat (Glasgow, 1994), pp. 146–68, at p. 146.

38 Cited in R. Bartlett, *The Making of Europe: Conquest, Colonization and Cultural Change, 950–1350* (London, 1993), p. 197.

39 *Ibid.,* p. 198.

40 *William of Poitiers,* pp. xviii, 122–3; F. Pollock and F. W. Maitland, *The History of English Law before the Time of Edward I,* 2 vols (Cambridge, 1895; 2nd edn 1968) 1, p. 74.

41 *Orderic Vitalis,* 2, pp. 314, 318.

42 See below, pp. 133–4 for frontier societies.

43 Bartlett, *Making of Europe,* pp. 208, 214–15.

44 See F. J. Turner, *The Frontier in American History* (New York, 1902).

45 R. I. Burns, 'The significance of the frontier in the Middle Ages' in *Medieval Frontier Societies,* eds R. Bartlett and A. Mackay (Oxford, 1989) pp. 308–9.

46 R. Bartlett, *The Making of Europe,* pp. 60–84.

47 M. Strickland, 'Military technology and conquest: the anomaly of Anglo-Saxon England', *Anglo-Norman Studies* 19 (1996), pp. 353–82, at p. 354.

48 See above, pp. 118–20.

49 D. Power, 'What did the frontier of Angevin Normandy comprise?', *Anglo-Norman Studies* 17 (1994), pp. 181–201, at p. 183.

50 *Orderic Vitalis,* 4, pp. 120–5; 6, pp. 454–5.

51 Musset, 'Aux origines: les Tosny', pp. 45–80.

52 Golding, 'Knightly burials', pp. 35–48.

53 K. Thompson, 'The career of William Talvas, Count of Ponthieu', in *England and Normandy,* eds Bates and Curry, pp. 169–84; G. Louise, *La seigneurie de Bellême, x^e–xiie siècles,* 2 vols, *Pays Bas-Normand,* nos 199–202 (Flers, 1992).

54 David Crouch, *The Beaumont Twins* (Cambridge, 1986), pp. 60–2.

55 For example, the Paynel family; M. Chibnall, 'Monastic foundations in England and Normandy, 1066–1189', in *England and Normandy,* ed. Bates and Curry, pp. 37–49, at pp. 46–7.

56 Power, 'The frontier of Angevin Normandy', pp. 197–8.

57 J.-F. Lemarignier, *Recherches sur l'hommage en marche et les frontières féodales* (Lille, 1945), pp. 9–33.

58 C. Warren Hollister, 'Normandy, France and the Anglo-Norman *regnum*', in his *Monarchy, Magnates and Institutions in the Anglo-Norman World* (London and Ronceverte, 1986), p. 23.

59 *Ibid.,* pp. 29, 32.

60 J. Le Patourel, *The Norman Empire* (Oxford, 1976), p. 278.

61 See above, p. 121.

62 See below, pp. 143–4.

10

The later twentieth century: Church and economy

The Norman Conquest took place during one of the great formative periods in the history of canon law. Reforming decrees –
promulgated in a series of Church councils from the Council of
Rheims in 1049 onwards – spread slowly through the Western
Church. They had the effect of strengthening the ecclesiastical
hierarchy, beginning to free the Church from secular control, and
attempting to enforce celibacy on the clergy.[1] But while good
relations between Duke William and the pope were important in
planning and completing the conquest, it is difficult to decide
what changes in the English Church can be attributed directly to
the Normans. Brian Golding summed up one view prevailing in
1994: 'By introducing bishops and abbots from Normandy and
beyond, William may have accelerated the pace of change, but he
did not alter its direction'.[2]

A century earlier, the question had been much more controversial. It had been one part of a bitter ecclesiastical debate on the
condition of the English Church and the extent of its dependence
on Rome before the Reformation, a debate which was sparked off
by a Royal Commission on the Ecclesiastical Courts.[3] The
Commission's decision that 'the canon law of Rome, though
always regarded as of great authority in England, was not to be
held to be binding on the courts' in the Middle Ages, was
supported by Bishop Stubbs in a Historical Appendix to the
Commission. When in 1895 Maitland was preparing lectures on
canon law in England he found that the medieval evidence forced
him to a conclusion that ran against the accepted view. His
lectures, published later as *Roman Canon Law in the Church of*

England, argued that the law used in the English ecclesiastical courts was essentially the Roman canon law, and that the Church of England did not make its own law. He added that it was probable 'that in the inferior courts ... a law was administered that might in some sort be called customary since its main rule was the rule of thumb'.[4] This contention survived a storm of opposition from interested churchmen, but his main contention that the Reformation was indeed a revolution, not merely a hiccup, in Church law stood the test of further research by canonists.

By the 1930s, when Z. N. Brooke published *The English Church and the Papacy*, in which he argued that William I had not erected a barrier between the English Church and the pope,[5] Maitland's views were accepted as academic orthodoxy in the Oxford history school, once dominated by Stubbs. The 'further investigation' for which Maitland had called has led to some disagreement on individual points of interpretation, notably by Charles Donahue.[6] However in a recent outline of the debate, G. R. Elton summed up the discussion in the words, 'After close on a century it looks as though Maitland's conclusions stand. The framework for discussion which he constructed still holds up'.[7] There has been refinement of details within the wider framework of Church reform. Charles Duggan argued that as canon law was shaped and applied in Church courts all over Europe, 'the centralizing and decisive impact of the "Gregorian Reform" from the late eleventh century onward, and the publication of Gratian's *Decretum* (ex 1139), which marked the dividing point between the old law and the new',[8] were more important than the Norman Conquest in determining the relations between the law applied in the English ecclesiastical courts and the slowly emerging common law.

William the Conqueror's relations with the Church, both as duke of Normandy and as king of England after 1066 have attracted the attention of historians from William of Poitiers onwards. The Conqueror's first biographer not unnaturally described his hero's reforms as indications of his piety.[9] Later historians have tended rather to point to expediency as the driving motive in William's relations with the papacy – motives shared equally by Pope Alexander II.[10] H. E. J. Cowdrey looked a little more deeply at motives other than expediency, when he considered 'the underlying bonds of conviction and interest which drew the papacy and the Anglo-Norman kingdom together in spite of all the factors which tended to prejudice their good relations'.[11] William was at great pains to obtain papal approval for his invasion of England, signified by the sending of a papal banner for his army; and once crowned he allowed papal legates to hold councils at Winchester and Windsor in 1070.[12] Some earlier misinterpretations have been cleared up. The 'ordinance' or writ of William I on Church courts is no longer thought to have been an attack on the secular usurpation of Church jurisdiction, and indeed it attracted very little attention before the fourteenth century.[13] As in so many other fields of study, historians now tend to focus their attention on the pace of change over the years of the conquest. The developments examined have included changes in the king's share in the elections of bishops and abbots, in the parochial church system as wide territories served from minster churches were gradually broken down into parishes, and in the changes in diocesan administration and the organisation of cathedral chapters.

Before 1066 when, as Frank Barlow claimed, England in the main stood firmly on its past, the country had not been isolated from continental influences. Close commercial ties with Flanders and Lotharingia were strengthened by marriage alliances. Edward the Confessor secured the appointment to English bishoprics of two priests with Lotharingian connections, as well as the Norman, Robert of Jumièges, who was translated from London to Canterbury.[14] Harold Godwineson, who had travelled in Europe, recruited some canons from Lotharingia for the reformed house of canons he founded at Waltham.[15] After 1066 the speed of change greatly increased, as a result of William's appointment of bishops and abbots from Normandy and nearby provinces. By 1154 'the bishops and the majority of the abbots were of French ancestry, the lower clergy of Anglo-Danish', nevertheless 'acute racial tension disappeared relatively quickly in England'.[16]

Research on the parishes during the past four decades has shown that the changes owed much to the movements of reform in the Church, and possibly rather less to the influx of new lords after 1066. In 1959 Reginald Lennard wrote of 1086:

For a village to contain a church was no unusual thing, and in some districts only a minority of the villages were without one. But such churches were the outcome of a long process which was still incomplete. If the beginnings of the development can be discerned in the first quarter of the eighth century and perhaps even earlier than that, much still remained to do, and much was in fact being done, in the later years of the eleventh century.[17]

The change was from the provision of pastoral care by groups of clergy who served a wide area or *parochia* from a central minster, to the establishment of smaller parishes served by a single priest, which predominated from the twelfth to the twentieth century.

At all times the laity, whether the kings or the great magnates, had some interest in the appointment of clergy. The smaller units easily became proprietary churches, built and endowed by the local lord and apt to be given to members of his family. Some minsters were annexed as endowments for household chaplains: John Blair suggested that 'the communities of household priests may have provided a point of contact between the old centralised minsters and the new world of manorial priests'.[18] Similar communities of secular priests were established in pre-conquest Normandy, as Lucien Musset has shown.[19] Endowment of village churches by the laity also took place on both sides of the Channel. In Anglo-Saxon England, Blair described how the complex ecclesiastical or aristocratic centres were being 'fragmented into local manors, the land-base of a thegnly class'. Wills illustrate how, well before 1060, household priests were being provided with individual churches, which gradually acquired permanent endowments of land and some kind of independent status.[20] Any debate among present-day historians is now concerned rather with details of the changes, which varied regionally, and with the speed at which new church legislation penetrated to the regions, than with any attempt to attribute sweeping changes to the Norman Conquest.

Detailed research into the organisation of cathedral chapters has shown how changes, initiated tentatively in the first half of the eleventh century, gathered speed after 1066, but were often not fully implemented until the mid-twelfth century or later. All over Europe the organisation of cathedral chapters was changing, with the establishment of hierarchies of dignitaries and individual prebends in chapters of canons, some of which had previously practised a form of common life. In some English sees the institution (almost peculiar to England) of monastic cathedrals was retained; in these, bishops stood in place of the abbot as the nominal head of a monastic community.[21] David Knowles pointed out that six new monastic cathedrals (Rochester, Durham, Norwich, Bath, Coventry and Ely) were added between 1083 and 1109 to Winchester, Worcester and Canterbury, which had been monastic since the tenth century.[22] In the secular cathedrals change is now known to have been far more gradual than was once believed. David Spear's detailed work on Norman cathedrals makes clear that, though hierarchies of dignitaries had been established in many French cathedrals by the mid-eleventh century, the change in Normandy came slowly. It was most vigorous between 1070 and 1090, and only at Rouen was the chapter fully organised before 1066.[23] As for England, Diana Greenway's work on English cathedral chapters shows in impressive detail how their organisation changed slowly between 1066 and the mid-twelfth century or even later; and that there was no wholesale introduction of a 'four-square' chapter of canons dominated by dean, cantor, chancellor and treasurer.[24]

Perhaps the greatest, and certainly the most visible, change after 1066 was in church buildings. Even though some cross-fertilisation can be seen in the 1050s, particularly between the abbey of Jumièges and Edward the Confessor's new church at Westminster, it was dwarfed by the massive construction of new cathedrals, abbeys and parish churches.[25] Georges Zarnecki has made an important contribution to the debate in terms of Romanesque art, which, as he explains, should never be called 'Norman' – 'the term generally, though not quite correctly, attributed to the Norman Conquest'.[26] Romanesque art was well established in Normandy before the middle of the eleventh century, particularly in the abbey churches of Bernay and Jumièges; Normandy was already in touch with the creative regions of France, Italy, the Empire and Spain. England under King Edward was beginning to open the door to new influences, particularly those of Flanders and the Empire, through the appointment of foreign bishops to English sees. 'This would undoubtedly have resulted in the eventual development of the

Romanesque style in England'.[27] The new royal abbey of Westminster was already modelled on buildings in Normandy. As for art and decoration, 'the Romanesque style had, to a certain extent, influenced Anglo-Saxon art, but it was the Norman Conquest of 1066 which opened the gate to a stylistic invasion from the Continent'.[28] At the same time, when the Normans 'found themselves the sole patrons of the arts in England they became heirs to complex artistic traditions'. These included the Ringerike style from Scandinavia, which often incorporated mythical animals entangled in foliage, and strongly influenced book decoration. Zarnecki concluded that 'almost from the start the art employed by the Normans in England differed in so many ways from the art of Normandy that the term Anglo-Norman Romanesque is fully justified'.[29]

This epitomises an approach to the question of the consequences of the Norman Conquest that has largely replaced the older, more confrontational, debates of the nineteenth and early twentieth centuries. Hardly anyone now denies the artistic skills of the Anglo-Saxons (or Anglo-Scandinavians). Eleventh-century observers were impressed both by the wealth of gold, silver and jewels used to decorate churches, church ornaments, and vestments, and by the skill of the goldsmiths and silversmiths employed in their making.[30] But change was dramatically hastened by the conquest, and the resulting culture and society was different from what had previously existed in either country, or what would have emerged had the conquest never taken place.[31] Normandy had been a prosperous duchy; the kingdom of England was conspicuously rich. When the wealth of England was added to that of Normandy the great magnates, including the bishops, no less than the kings and members of the royal family, had the means to employ skilled craftsmen and masons from kingdom and duchy alike to outdo their predecessors in the scale and magnificence of their great churches, and the strength and even beauty of their castles. Artistic and economic changes were inseparably linked.

Almost every cathedral and abbey church was rebuilt in the late eleventh and early twelfth century.[32] The new Romanesque cathedrals in both England and Normandy owed much to the wealthy magnate-bishops who had been granted great estates in

England, and were exploiting them so as to maximise the income they provided. All the bishops who undertook to rebuild or enlarge their cathedrals, with the exception of Wulfstan of Worcester, were of continental origin. Geoffrey of Coutances, Odo of Bayeux, and, a little later, Roger of Salisbury, were important barons with immense personal wealth in addition to the resources which they enjoyed as bishops.[33] Others, like Walkelin of Winchester, Lanfranc of Canterbury, and William of Durham, whose principal seats were in cathedral priories, provided the impetus to build but shared the cost with their prior and convent. All had great designs. William of Malmesbury's comment on Lanfranc's new cathedral at Canterbury was, 'You do not know which to admire more, the beauty or the speed of construction'.[34] At Winchester, Bishop Walkelin's ambition was to build a church to vie in magnitude with St Peter's in Rome.[35] Durham, planned by its short-lived bishop, Walcher, and begun by William of Saint-Calais, was continued by his successor Ranulf Flambard, and by the monks of the cathedral priory in the long vacancies before Ranulf's election and after his death.[36] Remigius's new cathedral at Lincoln proclaimed his dual role as magnate and bishop: it was linked to the fortifications in the castle. Henry of Huntingdon summed up its character when he called it, 'a strong church in a strong place, a beautiful church in a beautiful place: invincible to enemies as suited the times'.[37]

The architecture often incorporated elements to conform to established liturgical practices. A. W. Klukas, for example, has argued that some features like the western extensions and aisled eastern transepts of Winchester and Ely were intended to provide subsidiary altars both for the 'secret places of prayer' adopted in the tenth century in accordance with the precepts of the *Regularis concordia*, and for the veneration of local saints.[38] And influence was reciprocal: in the liturgy some Norman saints were venerated in England, and English saints in Normandy;[39] in architecture, the development of ribbed stone vaults, pioneered in England, soon appeared in parish churches in Normandy.[40] It would be difficult, if not impossible, to make a convincing case for the Norman Conquest as an unalloyed artistic disaster for England. Unquestionably, however, it speeded up and modified the changes.

Economic developments, like those in the Church, need to be seen in their European setting. All over Europe broad economic changes were taking place from about the tenth to the end of the twelfth century. A slow rise in population, not yet fully explained, was accompanied by advances of cultivation into woodland and waste. Both England and Normandy were affected by this change, and by a marked stimulus to trade. It could be said of Normandy no less than of England that 'elements of a money economy had penetrated deep into society', even if the basis of the economy was agrarian. The advance of cultivation into the waste made it possible to support a growing population, and one that included elements significantly above subsistence level.[41] No serious historian would now assert either that England was isolated from Europe, or that Normandy was economically backward, before 1066. But it is still not easy to determine how far the quickening of economic activity at the end of the eleventh century was due to general movements, and how far to the effects of the Norman Conquest.

The spectacular rise of new buildings that impressed contemporaries certainly owed its stimulus to the conquest. Castles, like cathedrals, were a visible expression of Norman power, and later generations were to take them as symbols of Norman tyranny.[42] The demand for labour and building materials had far-reaching consequences. The earliest castles, hastily erected as the Norman armies secured their hold on the country, were of the motte-and-bailey type, 'of which the dominant feature was the great flat-topped mound or "motte", encircled by a ditch, and with a kidney-shaped enclosure or "bailey" on one side. Both motte and bailey were protected by timber palisades, and the former was normally surmounted by a wooden tower'.[43] The bailey sheltered the horses of the defenders as well as protecting the bridge or stairway which gave access to the motte. In the first few years the only stone castle building was at Colchester and the Tower of London, both of which were fortress-palaces; in both the builders were able to use some Roman materials.[44] So initially the greatest demand was for unskilled labour, much of which was provided by the traditional services due from every man in King Edward's day, and converted by King William from *burh-bot* to *castle-work*.[45] There was a further impact on the local economy because of houses pulled down in towns to make room for castles, and encroachment on village fields when village sites were chosen. In time more castles were needed to house new Norman lords. Although many of the seigniorial residences known as 'castles' may have been at first similar in type to the fortified residences of pre-conquest king's thegns,[46] there were more of them, and many were soon enlarged to provide more spacious living quarters. The Norman castle at Castle Acre, with its two first-floor halls and surrounded by substantial earthworks, has been described by recent excavators as 'a country-house'.[47] And the later royal stone castles such as Orford, which was designed as both a base for the sheriffs of Norfolk and Suffolk and a staging post for the king and members of his household, provided comfortable living quarters for an upwardly mobile class of administrators, as well as being symbols of royal authority.[48] Cathedral building affected the economy in different ways from the castles; more skilled craftsmen were needed, and stone had to be transported by land or water. All this (except very occasionally when pilgrim fervour provided volunteers) had to be paid for.

It is not surprising that a debate is in progress about the impact of building on the economy. J. C. Holt made a strong case for Norman building having 'refurbished the economy of England' as well as being 'an expression of dominance'.[49] Richard Britnell, on the other hand, looking at the long-term process of the commercialisation of English society, has some reservations about the way the economy was affected by the new building:

> The building of cathedrals, castles and bridges in the early twelfth century was a more prominent feature of seigniorial expenditure than it had been during the eleventh century, since this was a prevalent form of extravagance. Roger of Salisbury used his fortune to build lavish houses on all his estates as well as to fund building at his cathedral. But most large projects of this type had little lasting effect on local patterns of expenditure. On balance it is improbable that seigniorial castle outlay can have had much independent effect in structuring the normal flow of cash into the countryside.[50]

He does, however, emphasise the importance of change rather more than continuity in looking at the effects of the Norman Conquest.[51] On this question, particularly on the impact of the Norman castle-building on rural society and on the prosperity of the peasantry, Rosamund Faith emphasises change. This she finds to the disadvantage of the peasants.[52] Robin Fleming too suggested that 'William's tampering with ancient tenurial patterns, not only on the level of the fee, but on the level of the vill, had huge repercussions for the kingdom'.[53] Tenurial changes coincided with a widespread change from letting out whole manors at farm to direct exploitation of the demesne land; and this was certainly stimulated by the financial demands of the Norman kings.[54]

One of the most intractable problems is the influence of the conquest on the disappearance of slavery, which resulted from a combination of economic, legal, and religious factors. David Pelteret has provided a useful analysis of different interpretations,[55] from Kemble, with his emphasis on religious motives, through Maitland, Vinogradoff and Marc Bloch, to the most recent studies, which investigate the changing manors of a particular county, with their peculiar customs and individual histories.[56] Pelteret himself suggested that 'it was the traumatic blow to the body politic delivered by the Norman conquest that provided the new lords with the power to ignore distinctions between slave and free among the peasantry'. Economic growth, accompanied by social destabilisation, was clearly important; he concluded, however, that 'the investigation of peasant social structures has not led to a consensus'.[57] The influence of the common law in England, which resulted by the thirteenth century in the exclusion of men and women of villein status from the royal courts, and referred their property disputes to the manorial courts, was one aspect of the changes in peasant status peculiar to England.[58]

Numerous trading centres existed in towns and villages in the tenth and early eleventh centuries.[59] Unfortunately they are inadequately documented. Britnell has suggested that 'the development of formal markets in England and in the rest of western Europe was inseparable from the exercise of power and the creation of law', and that in the period from 1000 to 1180,

> legal concepts relating to markets and fairs had yet to be clarified .... The law relating to markets and fairs was defined only gradually to the point where, in the thirteenth century, kings claimed the right to suppress those that operated without licence, and landlords took

their neighbours to court to suppress rival concerns.[60]

As in much in this period, lordship played a part, but its part can no longer be adequately explained, as it was half a century or more ago, as 'the crystallisation of the feudal system'.[61] The king's initiative in licensing markets was royal and public rather than seigniorial. As Britnell suggested,

> For the crown to have the right to order the suppression of illegal markets and fairs the criteria of legality had to be explicit and generally understood. So the legal concept of a market or a fair ... was built upon a variety of notions of public and private rights and duties. It was the product of a long historical development.[62]

Miller and Hatcher too looked at the long-term changes in trade and manufacture, and cautiously allowed a perceptible difference after the Norman Conquest:

> Ultimately the Norman Conquest served to strengthen the economic tendencies which had been at work in England since the late ninth century: urban growth, increased specialization in trade and manufacture, more production (including more agricultural production) directed towards markets .... But it is difficult to measure how far the tendencies had gone at different points.[63]

If there is any general consensus on economic development, it is that England was moving slowly in the same direction as other parts of western Europe, but that change was hastened by conditions brought about through the Norman Conquest.

On the question of currency and coinage there has never been any serious doubt. As Mark Blackburn summed up the situation, 'the late Anglo-Saxon system of coinage introduced by Edgar ..., which was the most sophisticated in Europe, was adopted *en bloc* by the Norman kings'.[64] In Anglo-Saxon England mints were strictly controlled; the silver content of the coins was uniformly high, and no foreign currency was allowed to circulate in England. The coinage was a valuable stimulus to trade, and an important source of royal taxation. The coin type was changed every few years, and moneyers were charged a fee for reminting as well as an annual payment for their office. Whereas William the Conqueror had replaced English by Norman officials in his central administration within less than a decade, he retained the goldsmiths: they were the group who most successfully weathered the conquest and continued to flourish. A goldsmith such as Deorman of London, who was apparently descended from an English thegn, retained his family's lands and office.[65] So currency continuity in the first years of the conquest cannot be questioned. Later changes in monetary control have mostly been treated as royal policy, and this is more open to challenge. Recently some historians have rightly emphasised the influence of changes affecting the whole of Europe. Peter Spufford's work on the coinages brings out the consequences of the serious shortage of silver in late eleventh- and early twelfth-century Europe, until the discovery in the 1160s of plentiful supplies of silver ores at Freiburg near Meissen changed the situation.[66] Mark Blackburn, investigating the reason for Henry I's apparent abandonment in 1125 of the former Anglo-Saxon system of frequent periodic recoinages, places it in the context of the silver shortage and the debasement of continental coinages.[67] So although the changes in the coinage 'correspond with a period of intense administrative reform, starting in 1123', the general economic climate needs always to be borne in mind during the pre- and post-conquest period. On this subject, no less than the impact of the conquest on the social condition of the peasantry and on the commercialisation of society, debate is still healthy and active.

New statistical approaches to the economic sources are constantly being attempted, but how far a statistical analysis of Domesday Book can be effective in producing valid conclusions remains an open question. An attempt has been made by J. McDonald and G. D. Snooks, but their sweeping claims for their particular cliometric analysis were dismissed by J. Z. Titow as, for the most part, a 'stimulating intellectual exercise', but 'of doubtful validity and little practical value'.[68] J. D. Hampshire was prepared to recognise it as a 'valuable contribution to pioneer studies'.[69] He acknowledged that the authors had successfully demonstrated 'that Round was incorrect in stating that hidage was artificial and unrelated to both resources and area', while noting that Galbraith had already shown this in his *Making of Domesday Book*. Casting a historian's eye at the system of assessment and taxation revealed in the survey, Hampshire observed that

The whole system, as with virtually all aspects of medieval administration, diffused outwards and downwards from royal authority through the major estate holders of the shires to the minor landholders and dependent peasantry. It had the priceless advantage of being simple, yet effective, with a built-in degree of longevity, being based upon landholdings. Administrative costs were small .... The scenario erected by McDonald and Snooks ... would necessitate a vast administration ... and would require virtually an annual production of Domesday Book to regulate it.

He pointed out, however, that he had attacked a particular statistical model in the context of one problem, and did not argue that Domesday Book was not suitable for cliometric analysis. The field is still open for cliometricians to enter the lists if they wish to do so.

Notes

1 There is a useful general survey of the reform movement in the Church in Uta-Renate Blumenthal, *The Investiture Controversy: Church and Monarchy from the Ninth to the Twelfth Century* (Philadelphia, 1988).
2 Brian Golding, *Conquest and Colonisation: The Normans in Britain, 1066–1100* (Oxford, 1994), p. 146.
3 G. R. Elton, *F. W. Maitland* (New Haven, Connecticut and London, 1985), p. 70.
4 F. W. Maitland, *Roman Canon Law in the Church of England* (London, 1898).
5 Z. N. Brooke, *The English Church and the Papacy* (Cambridge, 1931).
6 C. Donahue, 'Roman canon law in the medieval English Church: Stubbs v. Maitland re-examined after 75 years in the light of some records from the Church courts', *Michigan Law Review* 72 (1974), pp. 647–716.
7 Elton, *Maitland*, p. 79.
8 Charles Duggan, 'Papal judges-delegate and the making of the "New Law" in the twelfth century', in *Cultures of Power*, ed. T. N. Bisson (Philadelphia, 1995), pp. 172–99 at p. 173.
9 The *'Gesta Guillelmi' of William of Poitiers*, eds R. H. C. Davis and M. Chibnall, OMT (Oxford, 1988), pp. 78–89.
10 Golding, *Conquest and Colonisation*, p. 147.
11 H. E. J. Cowdrey, 'Pope Gregory VII and the Anglo-Norman Church and kingdom', *Studi Gregoriani* 9 (1972), pp. 79–114; in *Popes, Monks and Crusaders* (repr. London, 1984), ch. 9.
12 *Councils and Synods with other Documents relating to the English Church*, vol. 1, pt II, eds D. Whitelock, M. Brett and C. N. L. Brooke (Oxford, 1981), pp. 563–79.
13 *Ibid.*, 1, pp. 620–4.
14 F. Barlow, *The English Church, 1066–1154* (London and New York, 1979;

2nd edn, 1992), pp. 22, 45–6.

15 *The Waltham Chronicle*, eds L. Watkiss and M. Chibnall, OMT, (Oxford, 1995), pp. xx–xxi, 28–9.

16 Barlow, *English Church*, p. 311.

17 R. Lennard, *Rural England, 1086–1135* (Oxford, 1959), p. 295.

18 John Blair, 'Introduction: from minster to parish Church', in *Minsters and Parish Churches: the Local Church in Transition, 950–1250*, ed. J. Blair, Oxford University Council for Archaeology: Monograph no. 17 (Oxford, 1988), pp. 1–19, at p. 2.

19 L. Musset, 'Recherches sur les communautés de clercs séculiers en Normandie au XIᵉ siècle', *Bulletin de la Société des Antiquaires de Normandie 55* (1961 for 1959–60), pp. 5–38.

20 Blair, 'Minster to parish church', p. 6.

21 M. D. Knowles, *The Monastic Order in England*, 2nd edn (Cambridge, 1963), pp. 619–31.

22 *Ibid.*, pp. 131–2, 621–2.

23 David Spear, 'L'administration épiscopale Normande: archidiacres et dignitaires des chapitres', *Les évêques normands au xiᵉ siècle*, eds P. Bouet and F. Neveux (Caen, 1995), pp. 81–102.

24 *Fasti Ecclesiae Anglicanae, 1066–1300*, ed. D. Greenway, vols 1–5 (London, 1968–96); D. Greenway, 'The false *Institutio* of St Osmund', in *Tradition and Change*, eds D. Greenway, C. Holdsworth and J. Sayers (Cambridge, 1985), pp. 77–106; see also Everett V. Crosby, *Bishop and Chapter in Twelfth-Century England* (Cambridge, 1994).

25 Eric Fernie, 'Saxons and Normans', forthcoming in *Anglo-Norman Studies* 21 (1999); C. R. Dodwell, *Anglo-Saxon Art: A New Perspective*, Manchester Studies in the History of Art (Manchester, 1982); G. Zarnecki, 'Romanesque sculpture in Normandy and England in the eleventh century', *Anglo-Norman Studies* 1 (1979), pp. 168–90.

26 G. Zarnecki, 'General introduction', in *English Romanesque Art, 1066–1200* (London, 1984), pp. 15–26, at p. 15.

27 *Ibid.*, p. 17.

28 *Ibid.*, p. 18.

29 *Ibid.*, p. 20.

30 *The Ecclesiastical History of Orderic Vitalis*, ed. M. Chibnall, OMT (Oxford, 1969–80), 2, pp. 196–9; Eadmer, *Historia Novorum in Anglia*, ed. M. Rule, RS (London, 1884), pp. 109–10; Dodwell, *Anglo-Saxon Art*, pp. 118–19, 180–9, 202–5.

31 G. Zarnecki, *English Romanesque Art*, p. 20.

32 Richard Gem, 'English Romanesque architecture', in Zarnecki, *English Romanesque Art*, pp. 27–40; E. C. Fernie, 'The effect of the Conquest on Norman architectural patronage', *Anglo-Norman Studies* 9 (1987), pp. 71–85.

33 D. Bates, 'The character and career of Odo, bishop of Bayeux, 1049/50–1097', *Speculum 50* (1975), pp. 1–20; J. Le Patourel, 'Geoffrey of Montbray, bishop of Coutances 1049–1093', *English Historical Review 59* (1944), pp. 129–61; R. A. Stalley, 'A twelfth-century patron of architecture: a study of the buildings erected by Roger bishbop of Salisbury, 1102–1134',

Journal of the British Archaeological Association 34 (1971), pp. 62–83.

34. William of Malmesbury, *De Gestis Pontificum Libri Quinque*, ed. N. E. S. A. Hamilton, RS (London, 1870), p. 69.

35 Richard Gem, 'The romanesque cathedral of Winchester: patron and design in the eleventh century', *British Archaeological Association Conference Transactions* 6 (1983), pp. 1–12.

36 M. G. Snape, 'Documentary evidence for the building of Durham Cathedral and its monastic buildings', *B.A.A. Conference Transactions* 3 (1980), pp. 20–36.

37 Henry, archdeacon of Huntingdon, '*Historia Anglorum*', ed. D. Greenway, OMT (Oxford, 1996) pp. 408–9.

38 A. W. Klukas, 'The continuity of Anglo-Saxon liturgical tradition', *Les mutations socio-culturelles au tournant des xie–xiie siècles* (Paris, 1984), pp. 111–23.

39 M. Chibnall, 'Les Normands et les saints Anglo-Saxons', in *Les saints dans la Normandie médiévale,* eds P. Bouet and F. Neveux (Caen, forthcoming).

40 R. Gem, 'The English parish church in the eleventh and twelfth centuries: a great rebuilding?' in Blair, *English Parish Church*, pp. 21–30; Lawrence Hoey, 'The articulation of rib vaults in the Romanesque parish churches of England and Normandy', *The Antiquaries' Journal* 77 (1997), pp. 145–77.

41 E. Miller and J. Hatcher, *Medieval England: Rural Society and Economic Change, 1086–1348* (London and New York, 1978), pp. 25–6.

42 See above, p. 55.

43 R. A. Brown, H. M. Colvin, A. J. Taylor, *The History of the King's Works*: 1, *The Middle Ages* (London, 1963), pp. 23–4.

44 *Ibid.*, 1, pp. 30–2.

45 *Ibid.*, 1, p. 24.

46 Ann Williams, 'A bell-house and a burh-geat: lordly residences in England before the Norman Conquest', *The Ideals and Practice of Medieval Knighthood* 4, eds C. Harper-Bill and R. Harvey (Woodbridge, Suffolk, 1992), pp. 221–40. On castles in general, see R. A. Brown, *Castles from the Air* (Cambridge, 1989); D. Renn, *Norman Castles in Britain* (London, 1968).

47 J. G. Coad and A. D. F. Streeten, 'Excavations at Castle Acre castle, Norfolk, 1972–7', *Archaeological Journal* 139 (1982), pp. 138–301.

48 T. A. Heslop, 'Orford Castle: nostalgia and sophisticated living', *Architectural History* 34 (1991), pp. 36–58. For castles as residences, see also J. Le Patourel, *The Norman Empire* (Oxford, 1976), p. 315.

49 J. C. Holt, *Colonial England, 1066–1232* (London and Rio Grande, 1997), pp. 6–12.

50 R. Britnell, *The Commercialisation of English Society, 1000–1500* (Cambridge, 1993), pp. 48–9.

51 *Ibid.*, p. 48.

52 Rosamund Faith, *The English Peasantry and the Growth of Lordship* (London and Washington, 1997), ch. 8.

53 R. Fleming, *Kings and Lords in Conquest England* (Cambridge, 1991), p. 125.

54 S. Harvey, 'The extent and profitability of demesne agriculture in England in the late eleventh century', *Social Relations and Ideas*, eds T. H. Aston, P. R. Coss and J. Thirsk (Cambridge, 1983), pp. 45–72.

55 D. A. E. Pelteret, *Slavery in Early Medieval England* (Woodbridge, Suffolk, 1995).
56 *Ibid.*, pp. 4–24.
57 *Ibid.*, pp. 232–40, 253–4, 258–9.
58 See Paul Hyams, *King, Lords, and Peasants in Medieval England* (Oxford, 1980).
59 S. Reynolds, *An Introduction to the History of English Medieval Towns* (Oxford, 1977), pp. 36–9; G. C. Astill, 'Towns and town hierarchies in Saxon England', *Oxford Journal of Architecture* 10 (1991), pp. 112–13.
60 Britnell, *Commercialisation*, p. 10.
61 As in the lectures of Professor M. Postan in the Cambridge History Faculty.
62 Britnell, *Commercialisation*, p. 11.
63 E. Miller and J. Hatcher, *Medieval England: Towns, Commerce and Crafts, 1083–1348* (Cambridge, 1995), pp. 42–3.
64 Mark Blackburn, 'Coinage and currency under Henry I: a review', *Anglo-Norman Studies* 13 (1991), pp. 49–81, at p. 49. See also M. Dolley, *The Norman Conquest and the English Coinage* (London, 1966).
65 Pamela Nightingale, 'Some London moneyers in the eleventh and twelfth centuries', *The Numismatic Chronicle* 142 (1982), pp 34–50.
66 P. Spufford, *Money and its Use in Medieval Europe*, pp. 110–14.
67 Blackburn, 'Coinage and currency', pp. 72–5.
68 J. McDonald and G. D. Snooks, *Domesday Economy: A New Approach to Anglo-Norman History* (Oxford, 1986), reviewed by J. Z. Titow, *Economic History Review* 41 (1988), pp. 302–3.
69 J. D. Hamshire, 'Domesday Book, cliometric analysis and taxation assessments', *Economic History Review* 40 (1987), pp. 262–6.

POSTSCRIPT

> Postmodernism is a loosely structured constellation of ephemeral disciplines ... nothing if not syncretic, which makes it difficult to understand or even describe ... long on attitude and short on argument.
>
> Mark Lilla in *The New York Review of Books*, 25 June 1998

Once history had become established in universities it was constantly open to influences from other disciplines. This openness increased with the setting-up of combined degree courses and institutes of medieval studies. Historians have taken over and tried out the methods and sometimes the language of such subjects as economics, sociology and archaeology, often (though not invariably) with beneficial results. Archaeology in particular has made important contributions. Literature and the natural sciences were important influences even in the nineteenth century, and have never ceased to have some bearing on the writing of history. In the later twentieth century, however, academic approaches to literature began to take a new shape. Whereas in the eighteenth century Samuel Johnson had given as his opinion that history required at least as much imagination as the lower forms of poetry, and in the early twentieth G. M. Trevelyan declared that 'the appeal of history ... is in the last analysis poetic' and that 'its poetry does not consist of imagination roaming at large, but of imagination pursuing the fact and fastening upon it',[1] the followers of Jacques Derrida attempted to turn history into a form of textual interpretation. The more extreme deconstructionists and post-modernists were prepared to see history in terms of constructs open to almost infinite deconstruction according to the viewpoint of the writer. While a great many practising historians have remained untouched by theories that are essentially academic and literary, it is relevant to ask whether writers on the Middle Ages – and in particular on the Norman Conquest – have been in any way, even unconsciously, affected by these tendencies.

Recently Richard J. Evans, in his book *In Defence of History*, has taken a hard look at post-modernism in its various guises.[2]

While readily rejecting the extreme scepticism of some post-modernists, who deny the possibility of historical knowledge altogether, he suggests that post-modernist history, though not necessarily 'always as novel as it frequently takes itself to be,' has nevertheless 'both extended the range of historical writing and breathed new life into some old and rather tired subjects like the history of royalty and the elites, or the study of "big names" in the history of ideas'.[3] Among the new angles of approach that have, according to him, been stimulated by post-modernist writing are concerns with nationalism, or gender, or ethnicity. In opposition to this view, historians might reasonably object that all these topics had exerted some influence before post-modernism was thought of, and that changes in contemporary society rather than any new theories have influenced their new approaches to the writing of history. There is a great deal of truth in this, particularly in fields of study such as the Norman Conquest, for which so much detailed source material exists, and where new techniques of analysis provide the stimulus necessary to shake the writers of history out of dated interpretations. E. A. R. Brown launched her attack on feudalism by describing it as 'the tyranny of a construct';[4] yet long before this teachers of history had been insisting on the inadequacy of the concept of feudalism, and on the complexities of English and Norman society before and after 1066 without ever thinking in terms of 'constructs'. To the argument that even the most pragmatic historians may unconsciously have been influenced by arguments put about by post-modernist colleagues, they may reply that though historical studies have benefitted from some new angles of approach this is one so alien that it has left them unscathed.

The rejection by historians of extreme abstractions is to be welcomed by all who believe in the value and importance of history. New approaches will almost inevitably be made under the influence of changes in other disciplines. The chaos theory now supported by many scientists has already had repercussions in the humanities, most recently in Niall Ferguson's *Virtual History*.[5] This is a serious attempt to rethink 'counterfactual' arguments by investigating in a scholarly way what might have happened in order to understand what did happen. It is not new; to many, such questions are no more than parlour games or a subject for high-table conversation. Ferguson and his colleagues begin their imaginary investigations with the seventeenth-century civil war; but others have asked similar questions of the Norman Conquest. Among them was Maitland, who commented with charateristic wisdom,

> We can make but the vaguest guesses to the kind of law that would have prevailed in the England of the thirteenth century or of the nineteenth had Harold repelled the invader .... It is slowly that the consequences of the great event unfold themselves and they are not to be deduced from the bare fact that Frenchmen subjugated England. Indeed if we read our history year by year onwards from 1066, it will for a long time seem doubtful whether in the sphere of law the Conquest is going to produce any large changes.[6]

What Maitland looked for was an investigation of the whole structure of society to understand what happened and the way in which it happened. If 'virtual history' is imagined in this way, with a firm grip on possibility and a determination to see the changes as they appeared to those who lived through them and did not know what the outcome would be, then it can provide at least useful intellectual training for apprentice historians.

Conquest studies are very deep-rooted. Because Domesday Book provided information of some kind about land-holding and agriculture over a large part of England, it stimulates widespread interest in local no less than general history. The details are patchy; yet there are clues that, together with later charters and local surveys, make possible the reconstruction of family histories and sometimes of field systems. Local studies continue to be an abiding interest for learned amateurs from all disciplines, no less than for professionals. They are further assisted by the Departments of Further Education attached to many universities, and by the pioneering Department of English Local History established by W. G. Hoskins and H. P. R. Finberg in the University of Leicester. Historical geography, aerial photography, and landscape studies all make a contribution to the better understanding of conquest England at the local level.[7] Only for a relatively few individuals is there enough material for full-scale biographies; yet prosopography is making possible a deeper analysis of the social changes in various regions. Excavations of the sites of former castles and fortified residences tell something of the disruption of rural life that may have been caused by the invaders. Quite apart from the work being done in universities, studies carried out at local level constantly demand a readiness to consider any new interpretation that the sources seem to demand.

In the universities linguists and philologists, no less than art historians, numismatists and archaeologists constantly take a new look at both literary sources and artefacts. Even though Latin and Old French studies have declined in many schools, the translations of medieval chronicles and treatises and new editions of Anglo-Norman poetry have made a wider range of sources accessible to undergraduates and general readers. These works can provide a new angle on the interpretation of familiar sources. Richard Evans has suggested that 'one consequence of the post-modernist incursion into history is to make their emphasis on poetry and imagination seem contemporary once more, but poetry and imagination that are disciplined by fact'.[8] Yet historians, aware that David Knowles said in his 1954 inaugural lecture (as Regius Professor of Modern History at Cambridge), 'A historian may well, in his assessment of character, show the same genius of sympathy that we recognize in a poet',[9] will think that this approach has been contemporary for a very long time. And scholars have no need of prompting to work at providing facts of all kinds, to be disciplined in the new interpretations of the Norman Conquest that will surely be sought by the historians of the twenty-first century.

Notes

1 Quoted in R. J. Evans, *In Defence of History* (London, 1997), p. 250.
2 *Ibid.*, pp. 243–9.
3 *Ibid.*, pp. 243–4.
4 See above, p. 81.
5 *Virtual History: Alternatives and Counterfactuals*, ed. Niall Ferguson (London and Basingstoke, Hampshire, 1997).
6 F. Pollock and F. W. Maitland, *The History of English Law before the Time of Edward I*, 2 vols (Cambridge, 1895; 2nd edn 1968), 1, pp. 79–80.
7 See H. C. Darby, *Domesday England* (Cambridge, 1977; repr., 1979), the concluding volume in his *Domesday Geography* series, published between 1952 and 1977; M. W. Beresford and J. K. S. St Joseph, *Medieval England: An Aerial Survey* (Cambridge, 1958; 2nd edn 1979); M. Spufford, 'A Cambridgeshire community: Chippenham from settlement to enclosure',

Dept of English Local History, occasional paper 29 (Leicester, 1965), is a particularly good example of work produced in Leicester. D. Bates, *A Bibliography of Domesday Book* (Woodbridge, Suffolk, 1985), pp. 34–148, lists over three and a half thousand local studies bearing on Domesday Book.

8 Evans, *Defence of History*, p. 251.
9 Lecture printed in M. D. Knowles, *The Historian and Character* (Cambridge, 1963), p. 14.

FURTHER READING

Many of the historiographical works listed here have been mentioned in the foot-notes; they are grouped together here for convenience.

The Anglo-Saxon Chronicle, translation revd and ed. Dorothy Whitelock, with D. C. Douglas and S. I. Tucker (London, 1961).

Asa Briggs, *Saxons, Normans and Victorians* (St Leonards-on-Sea, Sussex, 1966).

E. A. R. Brown, 'The tyranny of a construct: feudalism and historians of Medieval Europe', *American Historical Review* 79 (1974), pp. 1063–88.

D. C. Douglas, *English Scholars* (London, 1939; 2nd edn 1951), esp. ch. 6.

D. C. Douglas, *The Norman Conquest and the British Historians* (David Murray Foundation Lecture, Glasgow, 1946).

Robin Fleming, 'Picturesque history and the Medieval in nineteenth-century America', *The American Historical Review* 100 (1995), pp. 1061–94.

E. M. Hallam, *Domesday Book through Nine Centuries* (London, 1986).

C. Hill, 'The Norman Yoke', in *Puritanism and Revolution* (London, 1958).

E. M. Jamison, 'The Sicilian-Norman kingdom in the mind of Anglo-Norman contemporaries', in *Proceedings of the British Academy* 24 (1938), pp. 1–51.

May McKisack, *Medieval History in the Tudor Age* (Oxford, 1971).

D. J. A. Matthew, 'The English cultivation of Norman history', in *England and Normandy in the Middle Ages*, eds D. Bates and A. Curry (London and Rio Grande, 1994), pp. 1–18.

Francis West, 'The colonial history of the Norman Conquest', *History*, 84 (1999), pp. 219–36.

Some of the Memoirs published in the *Proceedings of the British Academy (PBA)* give valuable assessments of the work of recent historians. See in particular:

G. W. S. Barrow, on R. H. C. Davis, *PBA* 82 (1992), pp. 381–97.

R. H. C. Davis, on D. C. Douglas, *PBA* 69 (1983), pp. 513–42.

J. C. Holt, on J. Le Patourel, *PBA* 71 (1985), pp. 583–96.

R. W. Southern, on V. H. Galbraith, *PBA* 64 (1978), pp. 397–425.

See also V. H. Galbraith on Sir Frank Stenton, *American Historical Review* 76 (1971), pp. 1116–23.

INDEX

his *Song of the Battle of
Hastings* 3
Guy, count of Ponthieu 10

Hale, (Sir) Matthew 34–5, 49, 97
Harald Hardrada 10–11, 32
Harold Godwineson, earl of
Wessex 9–13, 19, 32, 59–60,
141
his coronation 10, 12
Haskins, C. H. 70–4, 80, 84, 126
Hastings, battle 1, 11, 77, 87
Hayward, John 5, 32–3
heir, heiress 100–5
Henry, archdeacon of Huntingdon
17, 28, 127–9, 145
his *History of the English People*
4, 14–15, 17–18
Henry I, king of England 13, 93,
100–1, 103, 109, 111, 133,
150
Henry II, king of England 16, 30,
98, 101, 107, 110, 111, 133
his charters 63–4
Henry III, king of England 37
Henry VIII, king of England 29,
31
his break from Rome 20
Hereward the Wake 16
Hickes, George 43
Higden, Ranulf 20, 21, 130–1
his *Polychronicon* 4, 20, 21
Historical Manuscripts
Commission 55
historiographer royal 43, 44
history
Anglo-Saxon 57
as recreation 32, 46
constitutional 36, 57–8, 65, 70,
71
counterfactual (virtual) 156–7
economic 75, 104
family 157
feudal 44

legal 50, 65, 106
local 55, 75, 157
oral 2, 5
'picturesque' 56
poetic 5
political 65, 75
religious 65
social 57, 65, 69, 104, 106
vernacular 1, 5, 15, 16
Holinshed, R. 29, 30
Hollister, C. Warren 117–18, 135
Holt, J. C. (Sir John) 50, 75, 80,
83, 102–3, 116, 147
homage 49, 83, 99, 102–3, 135
in the marches 119, 135
honours (feudal) 73
household 107–8
knights 80
military 85
royal 85
troops 62–3, 102
Hume, David 46–7, 50, 75

imperialism, 81, 116, 121
inheritance 98, 100–1
Inns of Court 31, 34, 49
inquisitions, sworn 92
institutions 36, 92
Anglo-Saxon 60
English 57, 74, 90
feudal 72
German 58
Norman 62, 70, 74, 90
Ireland 2, 117, 120, 132–3
Italy, Normans in 72, 74

James I, king of England 33
James II, king of England 42
Johnson, Samuel 48, 155
John Trevisa 21, 131
juries 16, 92
justice, defect of 93
justices of the peace 32
justiciarship 110–11

Lightning Source UK Ltd.
Milton Keynes UK
UKOW01f0923030816

279858UK00001B/4/P